SPEEDPRO SERIES

HOW TO MODIFY VOLKSWAGEN

BEETLE

SUSPENSION, BRAKES & CHASSIS
FOR HIGH PERFORMANCE

This book is dedicated to Gillian – the only person I know who can build a kit-car with a single can of WD40.

Other Veloce publications -

Colour Family Album Series
Alfa Romeo by Andrea & David Sparrow
Bubblecars & Microcars by Andrea & David Sparrow
Bubblecars & Microcars, More by Andrea & David Sparrow
Citroen 2CV by Andrea & David Sparrow
Citroen DS by Andrea & David Sparrow
Fiat & Abarth 500 & 600 by Andrea & David Sparrow
Lambretta by Andrea & David Sparrow
Motor Scooters by Andrea & David Sparrow
Porsche by Andrea & David Sparrow
Triumph Sportscars by Andrea & David Sparrow
Vespa by Andrea & David Sparrow
VW Beetle by Andrea & David Sparrow
VW Beetle/Bug, Custom by Andrea & David Sparrow
VW Bus, Camper, Van & Pick-up by Andrea & David Sparrow

SpeedPro Series
How to Blueprint & Build a 4-Cylinder Engine Short Block for High Performance by Des Hammill
How to Build a V8 Engine Short Block for High Performance by Des Hammill
How to Build & Power Tune Weber DCOE & Dellorto DHLA Carburetors 2nd edition by Des Hammill
How to Build & Power Tune Harley-Davidson 1340 Evolution Engines by Des Hammill
How to Build & Power Tune Distributor-type Ignition Systems by Des Hammill
How to Build, Modify & Power Tune Cylinder Heads 2nd edition by Peter Burgess
How to Choose & Time Camshafts for Maximum Power by Des Hammill
How to Build and Modify Sportscar/Kitcar Suspension and Brakes by Des Hammill
How to Give your MGB V8 Power Updated & Revised Edition by Roger Williams
How to Plan & Build a Fast Road Car by Daniel Stapleton
How to Power Tune BMC/BL/Rover 998cc A-Series Engines by Des Hammill
How to Power Tune BMC/BL/Rover 1275cc A-Series Engines by Des Hammill
How to Power Tune the MGB 4-Cylinder Engine by Peter Burgess
How to Power Tune the MG Midget & Austin-Healey Sprite for Road & Track by Daniel Stapleton
How to Power Tune Alfa Romeo Twin Cam Engines by Jim Kartalamakis
How to Power Tune Ford SOHC 'Pinto' & Sierra Cosworth DOHC Engines by Des Hammill
How to Build and Modify SU Carburettors for High Performance by Des Hammill
How to Improve MGB, MGC, MGB V8 by Roger Williams

General
Alfa Romeo Berlinas (Saloons/Sedans) by John Tipler
Alfa Romeo Giulia Coupe GT & GTA by John Tipler
Automotive Mascots: A Collectors Guide to British Marque, Corporate & Accessory Mascots by David Kay & Lynda Springate
Bentley Continental Corniche & Azure 1951-1998 by Martin Bennett

British Cars, The Complete Catalogue of 1895-1975 by Culshaw & Horrobin
British Trailer Caravans & their Manufacturers 1919-1959 by Andrew Jenkinson
British Trailer Caravans & their Manufacturers from 1960 by Andrew Jenkinson
Bugatti Type 40 by Barrie Price & Jean Louis Arbey
Bugatti 46/50, Updated & Revised Edition by Barrie Price
Chrysler 300 - America's Most Powerful Car by Robert Ackerson
Cobra - The Real Thing! by Trevor Legate
Cortina - Ford's Best Seller by Graham Robson
Daimler SP250 'Dart' by Brian Long
Datsun/Nissan 280ZX & 300ZX by Brian Long
Datsun Z - From Fairlady to 280Z by Brian Long
Dune Buggy Handbook, The by James Hale
Fiat & Abarth 124 Spider & Coupe by John Tipler
Fiat & Abarth 500 & 600 (revised edition) by Malcolm Bobbitt
Ford F100/F150 Pick-up by Robert Ackerson
Jaguar XJ-S by Brian Long
Jim Redman - Six Times World Motorcycle Champion by Jim Redman
Grey Guide, The by Dave Thornton
Lea-Francis Story, The by Barrie Price
Lola - The Illustrated History (1957-1977) by John Starkey
Lola T70 - The Racing History & Individual Chassis Record New Edition by John Starkey
Lotus 49, The Story of a Legend by Michael Oliver
Mazda MX5/Miata 1.6 Enthusiast's Workshop Manual by Rod Grainger & Pete Shoemark
Mazda MX5/Miata 1.8 Enthusiast's Workshop Manual by Rod Grainger & Pete Shoemark
Mazda MX5 - Renaissance Sportscar by Brian Long
MGA by John Price Williams
Motor Museums - of the British Isles and Republic of Ireland by David Burke & Tom Price
Mini Cooper - The Real Thing! by John Tipler
Porsche 356 by Brian Long
Porsche 914 & 914-6 by Brian Long
Prince & I, The (revised edition) by Princess Ceril Birabongse
Rolls-Royce Silver Shadow & Bentley T-Series Updated & Revised Edition by Malcolm Bobbitt
Rolls-Royce Silver Spirit, Silver Spur and Bentley Mulsanne by Malcolm Bobbitt
Rolls-Royce Silver Wraith, Dawn & Cloud/Bentley MkVI, R & S-Series by Martyn Nutland
Singer Story: Cars, Commercial Vehicles, Bicycles & Motorcycles by Kevin Atkinson
Tales of Triumph Motorcycles by Hughie Hancox
Taxi! The Story of the 'London' Taxicab by Malcolm Bobbitt
Triumph Tiger Cub Bible by Mike Estall
Veloce Guide to the Top 100 Used Touring Caravans by Andrew Jenkinson
Velocette Motorcycles - MSS to Thruxton by Rod Burris
VW Bus, Camper, Van, Pickup, Wagon (Type 2) by Malcolm Bobbitt
Volkswagens of the World by Simon Glen
Works Rally Mechanic, Tales of the BMC/BL Works Rally Department 1955-1979 by Brian Moylan

First published 2000, by Veloce Publishing Plc., 33, Trinity Street, Dorchester DT1 1TT, England.
Fax: 01305 268864/e-mail: veloce@veloce.co.uk/website: http://www.veloce.co.uk
ISBN: 1-901295-80-X/UPC: 36847-00180-3
© 2000 James Hale and Veloce Publishing Plc

Readers with ideas for automotive books, or books on other transport or related hobby subjects, are invited to write to Veloce Publishing at the above address.
British Library Cataloguing in Publication Data -
A catalogue record for this book is available from the British Library.
Typesetting (Soutane), design and page make-up all by Veloce on AppleMac.
Printed in the UK.

SPEEDPRO SERIES

HOW TO MODIFY VOLKSWAGEN
BEETLE
SUSPENSION, BRAKES & CHASSIS
FOR HIGH PERFORMANCE

James Hale

VELOCE PUBLISHING PLC
PUBLISHERS OF FINE AUTOMOTIVE BOOKS

Contents

Introduction & acknowledgements 7
Introduction 7
Acknowledgements 10
Workshop procedures, safety, and
    tools 11
Workshop procedures and safety ... 11
Tools 12

Chapter 1 Chassis, suspension &
    brake design 14
The chassis 14
Steering gear 17
Brakes 17
Suspension 18
Front suspension 18
Rear suspension 19
Later versions 21

Chapter 2 Front suspension &
    brakes 23
King and linkpin front suspension ... 23
Disc brake conversions for king and
    linkpin suspension 24
King and linkpin suspension and
    brake maintenance 26
Lowering or raising king and linkpin

front suspension 28
The steering gearbox 31
Torsion-bars 31
Track-rods 33
Custom and Speed Parts disc brake
    system 35
Porsche 356 brake parts 36
Renewing brake shoes, wheel
    cylinders and bearings 38
Ball-joint front suspension 39
Ball-joint maintenance 40
Dismantling ball-joint suspension and
    overhauling brakes 41
Front shock absorbers 42
Fitting disc brakes 43
Renovating calipers 46
Aftermarket calipers 47
Calipers from other vehicles 47
Porsche components 48
Using five-bolt drums 50
Raising or lowering ball-joint
    front suspension 51

Chapter 3 Rear suspension &
    brakes 55
Swing-axle suspension 55

Improving handling with swing-axle
    suspension 56
Adjustable spring-plates 60
Urethane bushes 61
Solid mounts 63
Rear brakes 64
Replacing brake shoes 67
Fitting rear disc brakes 68
Oil seals 69
Fitting calipers and discs 70
Axle gaiters 71
Transmission oil 72
Independent Rear Suspension 72
Replacing CV joints 74
Standard units 74
Uprated units 75
Fitting Porsche stub-axles to Beetle
A-arms 75
Fitting Porsche 944 rear disc brakes 76
Removing the Porsche rear suspension
    and brakes 77
The handbrake 79
Porsche brakes 79
Anti-roll (anti-sway) bars 80
Tyre clearance 81
Obtaining parts.............................. 81

4

Chapter 4 The chassis **83**
Removing the VW Beetle
  bodyshell 84
1302/03 Beetles 85
Shortening the floorpan 86
Cutting the chassis 90
Welding the chassis 92
Modifying the shortened chassis 92
Cables 93
Swing-axle to IRS conversion 94
Frame-Head Swap 96
Beetle cables and pedal
  assemblies 97

Accelerator cables 97
Handbrake cables 97
Heater cables 97
Clutch cable and pedal assembly 98
Hydraulic clutches 99
Gearshifters and locking shifters .. 100
The 'Quickshift' kit 100
Gearshift locks 101
Conclusion 102

Appendix 1 Suppliers **104**
UK & EU Suppliers 104
US Suppliers 105

Appendix 2 Chassis numbers &
  transmission codes **107**
VW Beetle Chassis Numbers
  1940 – 1968 108
VW Beetle Chassis Numbers
  1969 – 1986 109
Transmission codes 110

Glossary of terms **111**

Index **126**

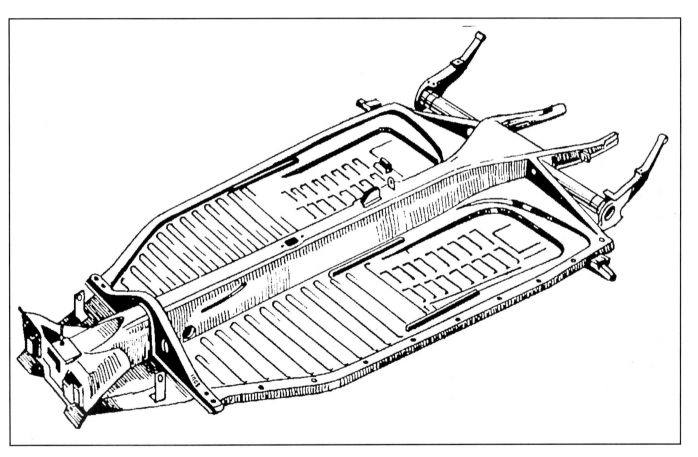

Veloce *SpeedPro* books -

ISBN 1 901295 45 1

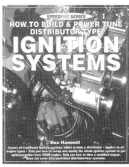

ISBN 1 874105 76 6

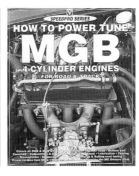

ISBN 1 874105 61 8

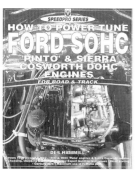

ISBN 1 874105 81 2

ISBN 1 901295 73 7

ISBN 1 901295 64 8

ISBN 1 901295 62 1

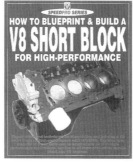

ISBN 1 874105 70 7

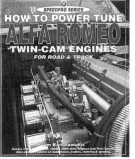

ISBN 1 874105 44 8

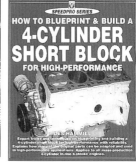

ISBN 1 874105 85 5

ISBN 1 874105 88 X

ISBN 1 901295 26 5

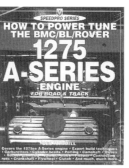

ISBN 1 901295 07 9

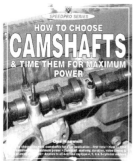

ISBN 1 901295 19 2

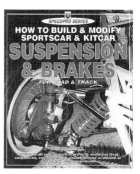

ISBN 1 901295 08 7

ISBN 1 874105 60 X

ISBN 1 901295 76 1

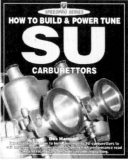

ISBN 1 901295 14 1

ISBN 1 901295 80 X

ISBN 1 901295 63 X

- more on the way!

Introduction & acknowledgements

INTRODUCTION

Like that of the Coke bottle, the shape of the VW Beetle is one of the most recognizable in the world. So many millions have been made since mass production began after the Second World War that it has had a huge impact on motoring culture.

Even the least mechanically inclined person knows that the Beetle's engine is at the back, and the distinctive sound of the air-cooled, flat-four engine is unmistakable. Production of the Beetle has continued to the present day at VW's Mexican plant, whilst VW in Europe has acknowledged the heritage of this landmark design by launching an all-new Beetle in the late 1990s, with a front-mounted and water-cooled engine.

With so many examples having been built during the car's long production life, the Beetle has inevitably attracted enthusiasts the world over wishing to modify, tune, customise and generally tinker with it. Aftermarket and tuning parts suppliers have all contributed to the possibilities of enhancing the original Porsche design, and a plethora of performance parts have been made available since the

The unique design and affordable price of the Volkswagen Beetle made it the best-selling car of all time. (Courtesy Beaulieu Picture Library).

Beetle suspensions, engines and gearboxes have found their way into numerous specials and racing cars, such as the Formula Vee class. (Courtesy Robin Wager).

The Beetle has proved a serious competitor in many forms of motorsport: on the track, at trials and hill-sprints. (Courtesy John Jackson).

The Beetle chassis provides the perfect platform on which to base glassfibre-bodied kit cars, such as the ever-popular dune buggy. (Courtesy Robin Wager).

The design allows the whole bodyshell to be completely removed from the unitary floorpan and running gear, as this publicity shot shows. (Courtesy ANWB).

1950s, many of which are designed to maximise the power output of the humble flat-four engine. With the Beetle becoming a serious contender in motorsport as diverse as autocross, Formula Vee and drag racing, this was, perhaps, inevitable.

A profusion of books covering the specialist area of Beetle engine tuning have also been published over the years, and with such a wealth of material available there was little point in duplicating what already exists. I have, therefore, approached this book with a different viewpoint.

My own interest in VWs began originally through a love of dune buggies, those glassfibre-bodied fun cars that were part of the youth culture of the 1960s and 1970s. Buggies were essentially made from two things: a glass-reinforced plastic bodyshell, and the rolling chassis and drivetrain of a VW Beetle upon which the new body was mounted. The Beetle lent itself perfectly to being re-bodied: the flat chassis/floorpan to which was attached the complete front and rear suspension components, gearbox and engine, remained complete even with the sedan body removed. The body was almost an optional extra, the chassis being entirely driveable without it, as witnessed in several early factory publicity photographs. This unique automotive feature induced many coachbuilders and customisers to use the Beetle rolling chassis to underpin alternative bodyshells, and thus it became the foundation for a multitude of pseudo-exotic vehicles, as well as simply the less glamorous, home-made one-offs.

My involvement first with buggies and Beetles subsequently, rather than the other way around, resulted in an affinity for the VW chassis, suspension and brakes as an entity separate from whatever was attached to it. Whilst I ardently admire Beetle purists for the time and devotion they put into the restoration to original specification or customising their vehicles, I prefer to see the excellence of suspension or brake engineering on a Beetle or Beetle-based vehicle. The use of carefully chosen performance parts to make the VW go, stop or handle better is therefore closer to my heart.

I have also come to appreciate the great interchangeability of different parts available within the VW and Porsche ranges, as well as alternative component transplants available by sourcing from other marques and aftermarket suppliers. By being totally broad-minded about the opportunities this avenue presented, I have benefited by getting the best performance from my own cars at a realistic cost. Rather than viewing a vehicle as a 'complete' car, I have also tended to look at things in terms of 'individual' systems whilst working on them: this could be a brake system, an ignition system, a fuel system, a suspension system, or whatever. This has greatly helped my understanding of how these systems work. By working on individual areas of the Beetle, it also means that buying components can be spread out over a longer period of time, which helps when keeping to realistic and manageable budgets. Don't forget, though, that modification or changing of components may have a knock-on effect on other parts of the vehicle. It is important to ensure that work done in this way is not to the detriment of vehicle safety.

I wrote a series of VW-related technical articles for a leading VW magazine in the 1980s, working on the principle that others who wanted to know how to perform such modifications, and who had even basic mechanical skills, could knowledgeably and safely undertake them. It also led to the first thoughts about this book. For those Beetle enthusiasts, like myself, who wanted to find out about suspension, brake and chassis uprating and rebuilding, there appeared to be a lack of 'stand alone' information available without having to wade through the greater part of a book on VW bodywork restoration, or engine tuning.

The book you are now reading is not intended to be a definitive workshop manual – you should still consider one of these an essential 'bible' for many jobs. Nor is it aimed at those who build high performance racing VWs or off-road vehicles, as that is an area that would take up more pages than are available in this book alone. What is here, though, is a guide to those who are hoping to get the best out of their Beetle's suspension and braking, and are happy to tackle modification or maintenance jobs that are well within the capability of the home mechanic, without the need for specialist garage equipment. Where a special tool is required (or welding equipment in the case of dune buggy floorpan shortening), this is pointed out in the text.

If you are new to the mechanical construction of the Beetle, it is worth reading through the text a couple of times before beginning a job or purchasing components. Always aim to work to a budget you have predetermined, and never attempt a job if you feel it is unsuitable for your vehicle, or outside the scope of the tools you have available. Remember that your own safety and that of other road users is paramount, as you tackle jobs which will affect the driving character, handling and braking of your vehicle.

Finally, it is worth making the point that the scope of the book does not allow as much information on the 1302/03 range of Beetles fitted with the later MacPherson strut front suspension, as the earlier suspension systems. With the development of many high performance suspension and engine parts for these particular models (particularly in Europe, for street and race use), this is a separate subject for a book in its own right. The 1302/03 independent rear suspension is covered, however, as it appeared on not only the American-spec. Beetles from 1968 onwards, but also on the European semi-automatic Beetle.

I hope you will enjoy reading the book, and gain inspiration from it. Most of all, I am sure you will find something in these pages that will help you improve the handling and braking of your own Beetle. After all, driving a Beetle is one of the greatest pleasures of owning it.

Stay safe and have fun!

James Hale
Brighton, England

ACKNOWLEDGEMENTS

Despite the wealth of material already published about the VW Beetle, finding the right information, photographs and technical details needed for this book was every bit as hard as I expected it to be.

Thanks are due to the many Beetle enthusiasts, both private and professional, who saved me from the ever-present pitfalls that surround a project like this. Their photographic libraries, mechanical skills, and, most of all, their enthusiasm ensured that I not only completed the book, but totally enjoyed the experience too.

A big 'thank you' goes to the following for all their help. For photography: Mike Key, Malcolm Bobbitt, John Jackson, Robin Wager, Walter Bach, Henny Jore, Thomas Kelm at Custom & Speed Parts, Geoff Thomas at Autocavan, Johnathan Day at the Motoring Picture Library, Beaulieu, Paul Cave, editor *Total VW Magazine*, Ivan McCutcheon & Mike Pye at *Volksworld* magazine, Gene Berg Enterprises, Chesil Motor Company, Red 9 Design. For providing parts for photography: Howard Blakes and Justin Bishop at Wizard Roadsters, Spectra Dynamics. For helping me set up photo-shoots and general assistance: Bernard Newbury, Mel and Sandra Baker, Peter Brunskill, Paul Burchell, and Dave Palmer at Creative Engineering.

To Mike Ghia for allowing me access to his detailed information on adapting Porsche components to the VW suspension and brake system. To Simon Glen for sharing his extensive knowledge of the VW chassis numbering system with me, and providing cutaway Beetle photos. To Neil Birkitt for reading the draft text and offering constructive suggestions, many of which I have incorporated into the final version, as well as providing photography.

And finally, to Rod Grainger at Veloce Publishing for allowing me to indulge myself with this project in the first place.

James Hale

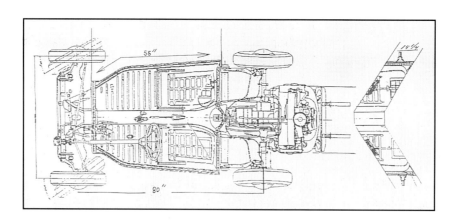

Workshop procedures, safety & tools

WORKSHOP PROCEDURES AND SAFETY

One of the things that makes working on a project vehicle a pleasure, rather than a chore, is a clean and dry area in which to undertake the work. A garage or workshop will not only keep you and the car dry, it will also help prevent the formation of rust on any of the vehicle components, particularly if the project takes a long time to complete. Whatever area you use should have enough space to work around the car, and should at least have a bench on which to work on components, and a dry storage area for tools and parts. If you have an electrical supply and use power tools, ensure these are also kept dry and are safely stored away after use.

Before starting work on your car, think about safety first – safety is common sense but, sadly, sense isn't all that common when you are ready to rush into working on your dream

car. Always disconnect the vehicle's battery strap, and remove the battery altogether if there is any possibility of a metal object falling across the terminals. Remove the fuel tank if you are using a heat source, such as welding gear, and place it outside of the working area. The same is true of brake fluid which is highly flammable, as well as corrosive to paintwork, and your eyes and skin. Obviously, do not smoke anywhere near a flammable liquid, or a fuel tank that may still have vapour inside. Never forget to wear appropriate safety clothing, including goggles if you are cutting or grinding, and gloves if you could hurt yourself on another part of the vehicle if, for instance, a spanner slips: skinned knuckles are no fun. Wearing a mask prevents the inhalation of harmful brake dust, and you should dispose of any dust carefully after working on drum brakes.

Also, when working on brake components, make sure that you do

not handle brake friction surfaces with oily or greasy hands as this will contaminate them and reduce braking efficiency. When replacing worn brake shoes, ensure that the replacements are made from asbestos-free friction materials for future safety.

Never work under an unsupported car – always use axle stands, and chock the wheels that remain on the ground. Never lift a car by placing a jack under anything other than a strong-point of the vehicle, or it could collapse on you.

The importance of thoroughly cleaning components before working on them cannot be over-emphasised. When replacing components use a copper-based lubricant on bolt threads, etc., to make future disassembly easier. Do not do this, however, on torqued components, as this will reduce friction and fittings can be over-stressed when torque is applied. In this case, use a light oil.

Always follow the manufacturer's

instructions carefully, and remember that changing component specification by modification is likely to void warranties. Make sure that you inform your insurers of any changes to vehicle specification, as this could affect your insurance in the event of a claim.

Ensure you read this book in conjunction with a comprehensive workshop manual, and do not attempt any work until you have read the whole book first. Make sure that parts you intend to use will do what you want, and will work in conjunction with each other – do not create a dangerous vehicle.

The publisher, author, editors and retailer of this book cannot accept any responsibility for personal injury or mechanical damage which results from using the book, even if caused by errors or omissions in the information given. If this disclaimer is unacceptable to you, please return the pristine book to your retailer who will refund the purchase price.

TOOLS

A kit of well-made tools will last a lifetime if looked after, and will pay for itself many times over. Always purchase the best tools possible within your budget, and shop around for the most attractive prices. Do not be tempted by cheap or poorly-made tools; the inevitable outcome will be skinned knuckles for you and a short working life for the tools.

For the type of work you will be undertaking whilst modifying your Beetle you'll need certain basics: a socket set, spanners (wrenches), screwdrivers, allen keys, pliers, internal and external circlip (snapring) pliers, and a fine drift. A selection of metric spanners will be needed including 10mm, 13mm, 15mm, 17mm and 19mm in open ended (crescent) and

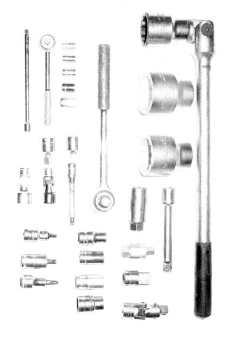

You'll need a range of sockets, attachments and extensions, including a 36mm socket on a 3/4in drive bar to release Beetle rear hub nuts.

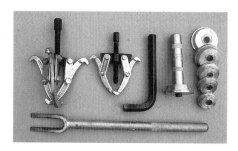

Bearing pullers, a large hex-key, a ball-joint separator, and a bearing removal and fitting tool are all great items to have in a toolkit for working on the Beetle.

ring (box end) form. A pair of 27mm open-ended spanners will be needed if adjusting the front wheel bearings on early model Beetles. Metwrinch 4WD double-ended spanners (or similar products) are great for removing nuts that have rounded off, as they work on the nut faces rather than the corners.

Metric sockets in a variety of sizes

The Torque-Meister tool is ideal for increasing the leverage on the 36mm rear hub nut, so that 30ft/lbs of applied torque will release the 270ft/lbs of torque at the nut.

will also be required. It's worth having a universal joint as well as a few extension bars to make life easier. A large 36mm socket on a long 3/4in drive bar is essential to undo the rear hub nut, and you can increase the leverage of this by using a length of pipe (scaffolding pipe about 6ft long is ideal), slipped over the drive bar. An alternative is a special, US-made tool called a Torque-Meister, made of tough 4130 chromoly steel which works on a toothed gear bolted to the VW brake drum. Turning the gear with a 3/4in ratchet at 30ft/lbs applies 270ft/lbs of torque at the hub nut to loosen it. Whilst a separate torque wrench should still be considered essential for your toolkit, this device is a blessing for any mechanic who regularly has to work on Beetle rear brakes.

Two other sockets that are necessities are a special splined tool bit that fits the hex-head bolts holding the IRS CV joints to their flanges, and a 45mm socket which acts as an ideal

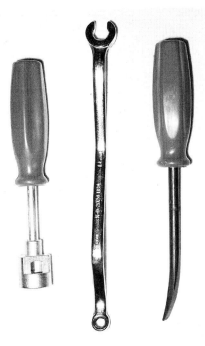

The ultimate VW Beetle tool. Although hard to find and store in the tool chest, it saves a lot of work when body removal time comes. (Courtesy Walter Bach).

Useful brake tools include: brake 'star' adjusters, a brake shoe retaining clip remover, and a bleed nipple spanner.

drift for fitting hub bearing races. An alternative to this tool is a special bearing race removal and fitting tool which features changeable flange sizes to allow working on a range of bearing sizes. The 1/2in socket drive ratchet bar is the most useful in any toolkit. It can be used with or without an extension, and takes all 1/2in drive sockets, including screwdriver or hex bits mounted in a special socket attachment. Hex bits also work with an impact driver, which is a useful tool when extra turning force is needed. Small 1/4in drive sockets are good in certain situations, such as stripping early disc brake calipers.

Some tools, such as axle (jack) stands and a trolley jack, can be rented and are necessary for many jobs when a vehicle has to be lifted

and supported safely. An inspection lamp is also a worthwhile investment.

Other recommended tools include a 19mm hex key or socket (which fits both the A-arm pivot pins and the gearbox plugs) and brake tools (an adjuster for quick turning of the brake 'star' adjusters, a brake shoe retaining clip remover and a bleed nipple spanner). For working on the MacPherson strut Beetle front springs, a coil-spring compressor is also a necessity in order to remove springs safely. Work on the rear suspension calls for a camber-adjustment protractor, if accurate setting of the suspension is to be undertaken and adjustement on both sides of the vehicle equalised: this tool can be hired. For work on ball-joints, separators will be required, and these come in a variety of styles, from units that progressively wind the joint apart, to the more brutal 'pickle fork' style which lever the joints apart but inevita-

bly damage the seals. The former appears the more attractive but, in practice, the latter is far more effective and often the only option when components refuse to come apart.

Don't forget a few pairs of locking-jaw pliers (Mole grips). Their locking capability is a godsend in certain situations, and they come in different sizes and jaw sizes such as straight, curved, or long-nose for different applications.

Finally, before you head for the workshop, consider having a range of pullers to hand. These are often overlooked, but can quickly resolve an otherwise impossible situation when a brake drum or bearing refuses to move.

If in doubt about the use of certain tools for specific applications, check with a tool retailer or manufacturer, or a qualified mechanic.

Chapter 1
Chassis, suspension & brake design

THE CHASSIS

The VW Beetle, originally designed by Dr. Ferdinand Porsche in the 1930s, is as unusual in its mechanical construction as it is in looks. The now familiar, rounded shape of the bodyshell was designed to form a complete, rigid structure when bolted together, with a light platform chassis acting as a stressed member. By designing the bodyshell panels with compound curves to make them both stronger and more aerodynamic, it meant that the traditional type of heavy girder chassis could be dispensed with.

From a servicing point of view, the combination of a separate chassis and body offers considerable advantages in the event of damage to the body or frame, as either can be

replaced independently.

The chassis - which is essentially a single backbone frame for torsional rigidity - carries electrically welded-in pressed steel platforms which form the floor, and on which the seats are mounted. These 'floorpans' are also

strengthened by the addition of a 'U' section around the edge, through which the body is bolted down. The central backbone tunnel, stamped to form the upper half of a tube and with a reinforced bottom plate welded to it, not only gives strength to the chassis,

The Beetle shape has remained much the same throughout its long production life. This is a 1953 model. (Courtesy Beaulieu Picture Library).

The oval window design, intended as a safety feature increasing rear visibility, replaced the earlier split-screen rear in 1953. The cable operated drum brakes, however, probably did little to inspire driver confidence. (Courtesy Beaulieu Picture Library).

Originally designed in the 1930s, the basic design of the chassis floorpan with suspension, steering, fuel tank and spare wheel at the front, and transmission and engine at the rear, still continues in production at the time of writing.

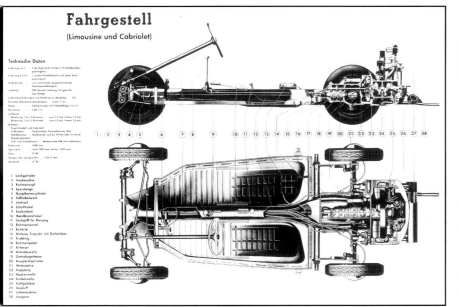

A German diagram of the Beetle chassis showing the control cable conduits running within the central backbone.
(Courtesy Stiftung AutoMuseum Volkswagen).

This early VW promotional diagram of the chassis and running gear features cutaways to show off the Beetle's engineering vitals.

but also provides the location for the accelerator, clutch and heating control cable conduits, the main fuel line running from front to back of the vehicle, and the gear linkage and supporting bush.

Handbrake cables also run in conduits from a point halfway along the tunnel length to exit at the rear of the chassis, and thence to the wheel hubs situated on the outer end of the axles. The handbrake lever itself, gearshift and heater controls are all mounted to the top of the central tunnel at a point within reach of the driver. The earliest 'Standard' model chassis also carried the rods and bowden cabling for the braking system inside the backbone, until the move to a simplified, and more effective, hydraulically-operated ATE non-servo drum brake system in the mid-1950s. The brake pipe running the length of the vehicle was then mounted next to the tunnel, but on the outside for easy access.

At the front of the platform, the central tunnel widens to form a frame-

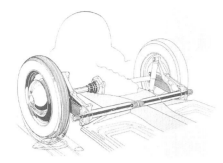

The torsion bars of the rear suspension locate within horizontal tubes at the rear of the chassis and, with spring plate trailing arms attached to the axle tubes, act as a swing axle design.

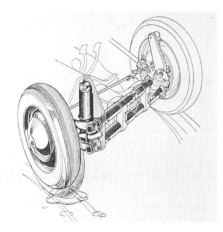

The Porsche-designed front suspension is very strong, and gives a comfortable ride on all types of road surface. A similar design was used on Porsche's own cars.

The Beetle's front torsion-bars were made up of flat steel leaves, one above the other, held at the centre inside each front axle tube. Cars of different years have different numbers of leaves.

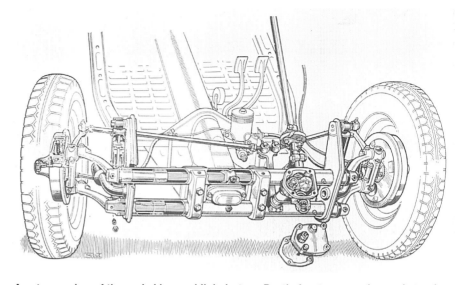

A cutaway view of the early king and linkpin-type Beetle front suspension and steering gear. This was later modernised to a ball-jointed design.

Racing events, such as the January 1954 Monte Carlo rally, proved the durability of the Beetle suspension and engine. Driver A. Prager drove a 1953 model. (Courtesy Beaulieu Picture Library).

head which provides the mounting points for the front suspension assembly. The front suspension - made up of two tubes containing torsion-bars, one

above the other - is positioned forward of the front bodyshell bulkhead, which allows for the fuel tank and luggage storage within the vehicle under-bonnet area.

At the rear of the chassis, the backbone splays out into a forked member, providing a cradle to support the transmission. The gearbox is attached to the chassis at three strategic points: one beneath the fork of the chassis and the other two on a removable support bolted across the very ends of the fork. Mounting blocks made of rubber-faced steel help insulate the inside of the car from engine and gearbox vibration. The coupling mechanism between the gear lever change rod and the gearshift lever of the gearbox is accessible through an inspection plate situated on top of the rear of the tunnel. Attached to the bell-housing end of the gearbox is the Porsche-designed, horizontally-opposed, four-cylinder, air-cooled engine. This was initially of 1131cc capacity in postwar 1949 'split' rear window Beetles.

Also at the rear of the chassis is a

pair of transversely-mounted solid torsion-bars with trailing arms, one on each side of the car. Located in strong tubular housings, and fixed at the inner end by a set of splines, the outer torsion-bar end is also splined, to accept the single trailing arm spring plate carrying the rear wheel hub and brake assembly.

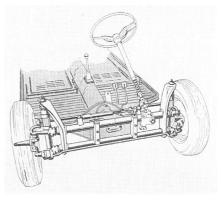

In 1966, the Beetle received a major overhaul in terms of body design, and suspension. Disc brakes appeared on the new 1500 model and were transferable to any other ball-jointed front suspension model.

The classic 1960s Beetle with king and linkpin front suspension, and swing-axle rear suspension. Many of the components can now be upgraded with high performance parts. (Courtesy Beaulieu Picture Library).

Steering gear

The steering gear was designed on the worm and sector principle (later changing to a worm and roller), with the steering gearbox mounted by a clamped section to the upper front torsion tube. Turned by the steering wheel, the steering column operates on the gearbox shaft via a flexible coupling. Inside the box, the helical thread on the shaft gives forward or backward motion to a splined sector shaft, and thus to the drop arm beneath the unit. Unequally divided track rods, with adjustable ball-jointed ends, transmit the steering movement to the steering arms of the stub-axle assemblies.

BRAKES

Apart from the very earliest Beetle chassis, which used cable-operated brakes, braking is courtesy of a hydraulic system, operating on all four wheels. Pressure applied to the foot brake – part of the pedal cluster situated to one side of the central tunnel – acts on hydraulic fluid in a closed system of rigid and flexible pipes via a master cylinder. In turn, this operates individual wheel cylinders within each brake drum, forcing a leading and trailing brake shoe within each drum against the metal drum friction surface. A cable-operated handbrake acts on the shoes within

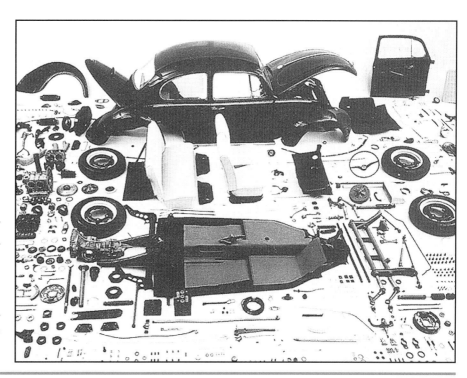

This VW advertisement shows the number of separate parts that went into the making of a Beetle. (Courtesy Walter Bach).

the rear drums only, when the handbrake lever is raised.

Front disc brakes first made an appearance on the 1500 Beetle in 1966, using the ball-jointed stub-axles previously seen on the VW Karmann Ghia model. These greatly improved the braking power of the vehicle, even though the calipers were only of twin-piston design. Other than on the 1500, disc brakes were only to appear on the GT model Beetle, and as an option on the 1300 model, as well as the later 1302S and 1303S MacPherson strut models. This allowed the Beetle design to be updated to meet changing performance and safety standards in its main markets.

1966 also marked the change from the large diameter 205mm five-bolt pattern of the Beetle wheels and corresponding wheel hubs, to a smaller diameter 130mm four-bolt fitting.

SUSPENSION

Front suspension

Apart from the MacPherson strut front suspension models first made available in the 1970s, all VW Beetles have torsion-bar front and rear suspensions. Use of this well-engineered torsion-bar system was, perhaps, unsurprising. The front suspension was Porsche's own patented independent system, providing a lightweight and compact design which allowed maximum space within the vehicle. The two bars are safely contained within transversely-mounted tubes to prevent damage, and allow more control and less wear than Porsche's earlier experiments with a single bar. The two parallel tubes running across the car are rigidly joined together and bolted across the chassis frame-head. Each houses a composite torsion-bar made up of a number of thin leaves, which are

secured in the centre of the tube to an anchor block by a dogtooth screw and locknut. This gives the effect of two torsion-bars from one assembly, making four bars in all.

Unlike conventional and heavy springs of the day, which gave a very firm ride and poor handling for a heavily laden vehicle, the VW torsion-bars stopped excessive wheel hop and reduced roll, giving a ride that was good over rough ground, yet soft enough to give a comfortable ride on proper road surfaces. They also ideally suited the lightweight vehicle as the torsion-bars - essentially a spring made up of straight bars of tempered metal – gave a rising rate springing effect. Fixed at the centre, the leaves of the bar resist the twisting force exerted on the other end as they are deformed by the motion of the wheels on the ground. The design ensures that the more the suspension is twisted, the greater the spring rate becomes. This characteristic of the suspension was a huge asset to VW when the chassis became the basis for the rugged Kubelwagen during the war and, more recently, on competition-winning dune buggies raced in demanding off-road terrain.

The earliest Beetle design used just four leaves in each torsion tube, pivoting on bearings inside each, but this was quickly increased to six as mainstream production began. To provide an even softer ride, post-1966 Beetles used a total of ten leaves, made up of four large leaves and six half-leaves within each set. The torsion-bars are mounted at each end of the trailing arms, secured by dog-tooth screws and locknuts, and to which the stub-axle assemblies are mounted.

Prior to 1966, assembly was designed to use adjustable link pins and bushes, horizontally-mounted,

The 1967 US–spec. Beetle was the last US model to feature swing-axle rear suspension, before safety legislation meant a move to the IRS design. (Courtesy Beaulieu Picture Library).

The body is secured to the floorpan, and to the front and rear suspensions, by a series of bolts around the outer perimeter. This is a 1968 model. (Courtesy Volkswagen AG).

with vertically-mounted kingpins acting as steering pivots. After this date, conventional ball-joints were used, with the top one mounted in an eccentric bush to allow adjustment to the camber/castor angles. Torsion-bar assemblies and trailing arms before and after this milestone date in VW Beetle production are not interchangeable. Spacing between the parallel bars of the early or later type differs considerably, with the frame-head of the chassis being designed to accommodate only either one or the other.

Shaped sideplates, vertical to the torsion tube assemblies, provide the top anchorage point for the conventional hydraulic telescopic dampers used at the front, though the post-1966 suspension incorporated bump stops into the units themselves, rather than being mounted between the trailing arms with a rubber block, as on earlier cars. To prevent roll, all Beetles from 1959 onwards use a stabiliser bar, attached to the lower trailing arms by rubber bushes and retaining clips.

Rear suspension

The rear suspension of the Beetle, with its solid torsion-bar design, is mounted independently on each side of the floorpan with the inner ends of the torsion-bars secured by splines, carrying the single trailing arm spring plates via splines on their outer ends. The spring plates bolt to the transaxle outer axle tubes which carry the rear

hub and brake assemblies, and feature elongated bolt-holes to allow for toe-in/toe-out adjustment. Inside the tubes run the solid one-piece axles which are driven at the transaxle end through a spade and socket type universal joint, whilst splining straight into the wheel hub brake drum at the outer end. Cheap to manufacture and with little maintenance required, except to replace the hub seals and axle gaiters which retain the lubricating oil within the axle tubes, the design does have one major drawback: as the rear suspension is raised or compressed, it describes an arc at the outer end, creating a high roll centre as the axle pivots at the transaxle. The design does not allow for any sideways movement to correct such camber changes, due to the rigid axle tubes. These adverse camber changes result in the Beetle having a feeling of extremely nervous handling at the rear on uneven road surfaces, and particularly so in the wet.

Modifications to this design came in 1967 with the advent of the semi-

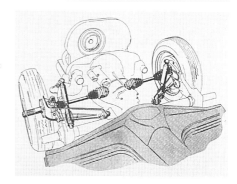

Independent rear suspension (IRS) used constant velocity (CV) joints in the axles to allow better wheel geometry and to prevent adverse camber changes during cornering and on uneven road surfaces.

automatic Beetle model, also known as the 'Stickshift' model. Unable to accommodate the revised axle position of the longer three-speed gearbox and torque converter, the conventional solid axles were replaced by a new design using a short, solid axle mounted between two constant velocity (CV) joints on each side of the car. The gearbox carries a flange on each side to which the inner CV joints are bolted, whilst the outer two are bolted to similar flanges forming part of the two short, splined axles running in bearings mounted within hub carriers on either side of the vehicle, and to which the brake drums are mounted. The CV joints allow for angular movement of the axle as the suspension moves up and down, and therefore offers vastly improved road holding by minimising adverse camber changes. Often referred to as a four-joint rear suspension or Independent Rear Suspension (IRS), the latter term is not strictly correct as the swing axle suspension was also independent, but

In Europe, the sophisticated diagonal trailing arm independent rear suspension (IRS) design was initially fitted only to the semi-automatic model. Widespread use on 1302/03 models followed later. (Courtesy Robin Wager).

The 1970 Sun Sedan was the US-market sunroof Beetle. It featured ball-joint front suspension and IRS rear for better roadholding.
(Courtesy Beaulieu Picture Library).

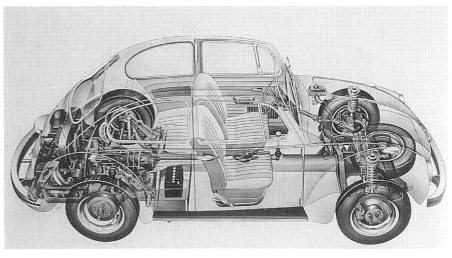

An illustration of the Super Beetle design. The model featured a modernised front suspension design, with the MacPherson strut suspension allowing more space under the front hood for luggage.

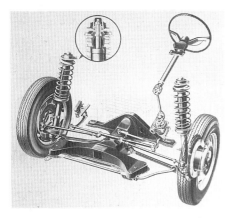

This illustration shows the MacPherson strut front suspension and the steering column on the later Super Beetle models, introduced for the 1971 model year.

Beetle chassis with engine, transmission, steering, suspension and wheels fitted. This is a 1302 model with IRS rear suspension, and MacPherson strut front suspension.
(Courtesy Simon Glen).

A cutaway Beetle showing the basis of the later design, including the safety steering wheel. (Courtesy Walter Bach).

The 1303 model was the last major development of the Wolfsburg-made Beetles. It featured a panoramic windscreen and greater interior space due to the curved, padded dashboard.

offered on 1300 and 1500 Beetles, but the IRS design was quickly adopted into the US-spec. model range from 1968 onwards to meet increasingly stringent American vehicle safety standards. The design, apart from minimising camber changes and allowing superior roadholding, provided another benefit – that of making work on the transmission much easier, as it could now be removed from the vehicle without removing the whole transaxle. This meant that all other parts of the rear suspension were left attached to the chassis, and the vehicle could remain on its wheels.

LATER VERSIONS

In a bid to modernise the Beetle, VW

the general designation has now become the accepted term to describe this design.

With the rear hubs no longer laterally located to the transmission, semi-trailing arm arrangements (also referred to as diagonal A-arms) were introduced to connect the hub assemblies to chassis-mounted brackets at each side of the transmission fork abutting the torsion-bar tubes. Pivoting on bush-mounted pins, the semi-trailing arms complete the job of locating the road wheels. Unlike the front suspension, the spring plate and diagonal arms aren't fully trailing and

give a small amount of toe-out to the wheel during travel. The sole purpose served by the axles between the CV joints is to transmit engine power to the wheels.

The semi-automatic option was

This shot of the underside of the Super Beetle design shows the IRS rear suspension and the radically different front suspension design required to mount the MacPherson strut coil springs, the control arms and the stabiliser.

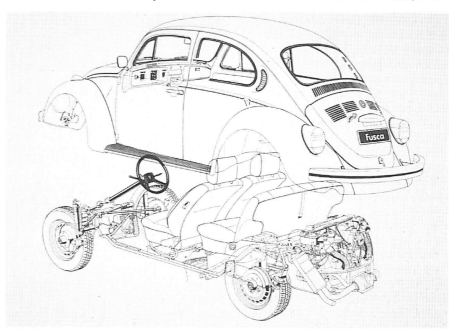

Brazilian-made Fusca Beetles represent the most up-to-date development of the original design. They have, however, reverted back to the swing-axle rear suspension, although discs are now standard at the front.

introduced a new model in 1970, with a radically changed front suspension design and updated overall look. The 1302, as it was named, had a larger front hood to give greater luggage space, and revisions to the front part of the chassis to accommodate the MacPherson strut front suspension. The rear suspension was the same IRS design as on the stickshift model which, combined with the modifications to the front, produced the most refined of all Beetle designs for roadholding. The 1300cc version of the 1302 design, together with the 1600cc 1302S, fitted with front disc brakes, provided greater driver comfort and luggage capacity but lacked the simplistic character and universal appeal of the earlier models.

A final version of the European-made MacPherson strut model Beetle appeared in 1972. Called the 1303, it was also produced in 1300cc and 1600cc (1303S) engine forms. Both the 1302 and the 1303 were known as 'Super Beetles' in the US to differentiate them from the more usual torsion-bar Beetles. Recognizable by its large, rounded front windscreen, the 1303 and its Cabriolet version also received the benefit of a rack and pinion steering design in 1974, just one year before the saloon version was phased out altogether.

As VW began to concentrate on the introduction of new water-cooled models, the Beetle saloon was finally taken out of German production in 1978, exactly one year after US dealers had ceased stocking it. The Beetle design has lived on in Mexico, however, as VW has moved its production facility to meet the needs of new markets. The design has reverted to the torsion-bar front and swing axle rear suspensions, though various bodywork and engine revisions have taken place to adapt the Beetle concept to meet more modern styles and regulations.

Parts availability has never been better, and ever-growing interest in the car has meant that there's now a flourishing aftermarket parts scene for both stock and high performance components to modify this once humble design.

How you decide to modify your Beetle is, of course, entirely up to you; let's take a look at some of the options available ...

Visit Veloce on the Web - www.veloce.co.uk

Chapter 2
Front suspension & brakes

To keep things in a logical order, I have started by looking at the Beetle king and linkpin front suspension design before the ball-joint type, simply because they appeared that way in VW production history. Some references made about procedures or modifications in one section may be applicable to more than one suspension design, and this will be pointed out in the text.

KING AND LINKPIN FRONT SUSPENSION

All VW Beetles produced up until July 1965 use a front suspension design featuring stub-axle assemblies swivelled on kingpins within kingpin carriers. The stub-axles are turned through the action of ball-jointed track-rods operated by the steering gearbox. The kingpin carriers locate the wheel

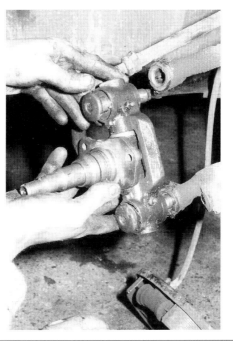

The stub-axle on early Beetles pivots on a kingpin within a shaped carrier. This also locates the horizontal linkpins attaching the carrier to the trailing arms.

hubs and brakes, and are attached to the trailing-arms, and thus the torsion-bars, by horizontally-mounted, case-hardened linkpins that run in plain bushes pressed into the carriers. The

outer end of the linkpin is located by a flange, whilst the inner end has a squared section that allows spanner adjustment. The linkpin is secured into the split-eye section of the trailing-arm by a pinch bolt.

The linkpins have helical grooves on their shanks (which engage the pinch bolts of the trailing-arms) so that turning the pin adjusts end float as it rotates. This adjustment, together with spacing shims of different thicknesses that sit each side of the linkpin bush in the carrier, sets the suspension geometry. The kingpin itself runs in bushes at the top and bottom of its length, mounted within the carrier, and provides the pivot on which the stub-axle rotates. Each kingpin carrier has two grease nipples which allow lubrication of the linkpins.

Providing components are well maintained and regularly lubricated, the system is very durable, though superior roadholding and ease of maintenance of the later ball-jointed

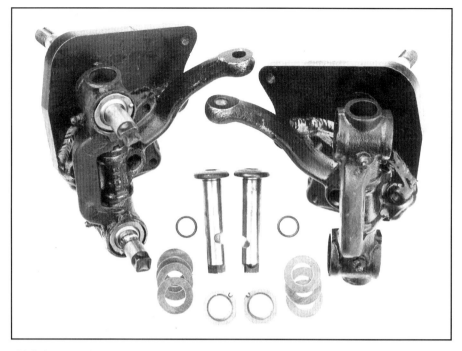

Linkpins use shims to set the correct suspension geometry. This JaTech setup allows the use of disc brakes, and lowers the suspension by 2 inches (51mm).

CB Performance forged 2in/51mm dropped spindles are available for both the king and linkpin suspensions (top) and ball-joint suspensions (above), and allow the fitment of high performance disc brakes.

Autocavan supply a 11in/280mm disc brake kit (using Golf GTi calipers) for early and late Beetle suspension types. This design retains the early five-bolt wheel pattern. (Courtesy Autocavan).

This Custom & Speed Parts disc brake design (for the early Beetle suspension) uses CNC-machined alloy hubs and brake caliper brackets, and modern ATE calipers. (Courtesy CSP).

This cross-drilled disc brake set up (for early Beetle suspension) from Neal, features race-quality Wilwood calipers and lightweight billet aluminium hubs.

design were the reasons for the ultimate demise of this part of the earlier Beetle suspension.

DISC BRAKE CONVERSIONS FOR KING AND LINKPIN SUSPENSION

Owners of early cars can undertake most of the maintenance needed to keep this type of VW suspension in perfect working order, and can also upgrade the design with modern components. In the 40-odd years since the VW king and linkpin suspension was first introduced, most modern vehicle designs have advanced with the addition of front disc brakes. This, however, was never an option on earlier Beetles, though aftermarket parts are now available to rectify this, and there are quite a few designs to choose from.

The designs can be divided into two types: those that allow the fitting of disc brakes by mounting the caliper to a special bracket attached to the stub-axle; and those that require that the entire stub-axle assembly is changed to one that has an integral bracket for the mounting of the disc brake caliper. With the latter designs, it's necessary to disassemble the kingpin carrier to fit them, and it is worthwhile planning on making this change whilst undertaking other work

This US-made CNC lightweight disc brake installation is ideal for lightweight vehicles such as dune buggies. A wheel adapter also allows the use of aftermarket wheels with different bolt or stud patterns.

CB Performance forged spindles (right) are much stronger than welded items (left) and don't push the wheels out. Good to know if wing (fender) to tyre spacing is an issue.

to replace the king and linkpins and their bushes.

Of the designs that require brackets, the most noteworthy are those by US manufacturer Neal, which have cross-drilled discs, race-quality, modified Wilwood calipers and original VW-sized, 205mm, five-stud wheel mountings on the billet aluminium hubs (these studs can, incidentally, be changed for 12mm Ford studs to allow the use of shouldered bolts). Also in

A CB Performance dropped spindle setup, with high performance cross-drilled discs and stronger linkpin bushes, can transform the braking capacity and longevity of the original design.

the US, Jamar produces a disc brake kit with cross-drilled discs and five studs. In the UK, Autocavan supplies a 280mm disc brake kit with high performance Golf GTi calipers for king and linkpin or ball-joint front suspensions, but fitted with the large five-bolt VW wheel mounting. Custom and Speed Parts in Germany produces a beautifully engineered five-stud kit using ATE calipers from a Vauxhall Cavalier. We'll take a closer look at this installation and its fitting a little later in the chapter.

Kits that require the complete stub-axle to be changed include the lightweight, US-made, five-stud CNC design using aluminium discs, which are especially suited to fitment on dune buggies. Also from the US is the JaTech dropped spindle design (also made for the ball-joint suspension, and in drum brake format), which uses a welded plate to reposition the spindles which then accept standard four-bolt replacement or aftermarket discs using stock bearings. Finally, CB Performance in the US offer one of the newest and best aftermarket conversions. The 2 inch dropped spindles (also made for the ball-joint suspension, and in a drum brake format), are new forgings with new, machined stub-axles to accept standard discs and bearings.

All of these give your Beetle a much greater braking capability. Discs allow a more positive, fade-free performance, and also have the advantage of being self-adjusting to take up pad wear. A secondary advantage is that some of the disc braked spindles mentioned previously have the actual spindle raised by 2 inches in relation to the steering arm. This allows an equivalent reduction in the height of the front suspension, and thus gives a lowering effect on the Beetle.

Apart from the improved visual stance of the car, this effect reduces airflow under the front of the car and makes it less prone to wandering in crosswinds. This aids straight-line stability and is one reason why cars used for drag-racing purposes are low at the front. Lowered or 'dropped' spindles do not adversely affect vehicle ride quality (which is a problem we will look at with other types of suspension lowering, where suspension travel is reduced and steering geometry is affected). Fitting dropped spindles ensures that the Beetle still drives as if it is fitted with stock suspension. The only drawback with such a conversion is that, unlike some other methods of ride-height adjustment, which we will cover more fully in the section on ball-joint suspensions, the suspension cannot be raised or lowered once fitted. The other problem is that some manufacturers of dropped spindles machine the spindles off the original assembly and re-weld them to thick plates between them and the stub-axle assembly, but 2 inches higher in their new location. This additional plate adds to the wheel track of the car and can position the tyres close to the fenders, especially if wide wheels have been fitted.

Those made by CB Performance - which are forged items with

chromoly stub-axles machined from new castings - are both narrower and stronger than welded items, and maintain the standard steering geometry. Their only drawback, should you decide to use them, is that you will need to drill and tap the mounts for the brake disc backplates, as they do not come with these. Backplates are important on a road car, so take a template from a VW stub-axle and get these attended to by an engineering shop.

Disc brake assemblies react very sensitively to wear on the spindles and stub-axles, and particularly on the linkpins. Therefore, even if you plan on fitting a disc kit that does not specifically require the complete strip-down of the king and linkpin assemblies, these should all be carefully checked for wear; it's far easier to replace components on an early suspension as part of one operation than to have to strip it down again later.

During the renewal process, it's possible to replace the standard bushings and pins with high performance components, if required. Stronger, aluminium-bronze linkpin bushes are available as aftermarket parts, and these are claimed to outlast standard units by over eight times. These can also be combined with through-hardened linkpins made from high tensile 4130 chromoly steel, and this effectively eliminates the weakest part of an early front suspension. These items are produced by companies such as Sway-a-Way. Although

Stronger aluminium-bronze linkpin bushes are available to replace the standard plain metal items. These can last up to eight times longer than the originals.

essentially for off-road use, they are equally practical on road cars and feature the added benefit of a fine threaded end and locknut that replaces the squared end of the stock items. This allows easier adjustment for steering geometry alignment, and effectively clamps the kingpin carrier and trailing-arms together for added strength, though the pin is still held in place by the original pinch bolt.

As stock kingpins and their bushes are rarely problematic, the use of aftermarket, high-tensile pins and aluminium-bronze bushes is not

Two 27mm nuts and a lock tab adjust the front wheel hub bearings. These have to be removed to release the front drum once the brake shoes have been slackened.

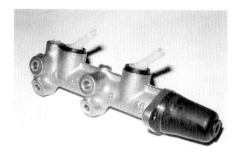

The master cylinder must be changed to a dual-circuit unit, with a residual pressure valve, if the conversion to disc brakes is made. Cylinder size is shown on the side.

necessary, although such parts are available. Whether fitting stock replacement king and linkpins or high performance parts, or adding a disc brake conversion, the process is much the same. All king and linkpin work must be done on both sides of the car, and parts are supplied in kits for that purpose.

KING AND LINKPIN SUSPENSION AND BRAKE MAINTENANCE

Firstly, jack-up the car at the front and safely secure it on axle stands, having applied the handbrake to hold the rear wheels. With the road wheels removed, remove the small circlip or split pin securing the speedometer drive cable from the nearside hub and withdraw the cable, then lever off the bearing dust cover. Inside, you will find the two 27mm nuts and a lock tab on the end of the stub-axle which adjust the front wheel hub bearings. Remove these and pull off the inner thrust washer before adjusting the brake shoes away from the inner surface of the drum and pulling off the complete drum. The brake backplate assembly can then be unbolted from the stub-axle mounting flange. The brake line can stay connected, unless you are planning a brake overhaul as well. The assembly should be hooked up with wire to prevent overstretching of the brake lines.

If the conversion to discs is being made, the brake fluid should be completely drained, as a new dual-circuit master-cylinder with residual pressure valve also needs to be fitted, together with a later fluid reservoir with two separate chambers, as found on Beetles from 1968 onwards. Changing to the more modern dual-circuit master-cylinder ensures that the brake system has a small amount of residual pressure when the pedal is released, to prevent air entering the system. A drilling in the valve subsequently results in the pressure dropping slightly to allow the disc brake system to be free of pressure when not in operation. If this didn't happen, the brake pads would wear rapidly through constant contact with the discs. The dual-circuit cylinder has two pistons, one behind the other, which control two separate braking circuits, one for the front and one for the rear of the car. This is a safety device, because if one circuit should fail, the other will still remain functional. Each circuit is fed independently with brake fluid from the fluid reservoir, and operates on one pair of wheels. The dual-circuit master-cylinder mounts in exactly the same way as the single-circuit version, but features different inlet port elbows, outlet pipes and brake light switch leads. A car thus equipped should also have the brake fluid reservoir repositioned from the wheel well to the side of the under-bonnet area. The brake pushrod, which is operated by the brake pedal, must also be adjusted so that there is a clearance of 1mm between the pushrod and the piston recess. The pedal stop (which is moveable) must be positioned far enough back to allow full pedal movement to operate the second circuit in the event of the first failing.

The metal brake pipes are unscrewed from the master-cylinder, and the hoses removed before releasing the unit. The two long screws in the bulkhead behind the brake pedal which attach the cylinder to the outer bulkhead have to be released and drawn back only partially, or the internal spacers will fall into the recess of the double-skinned bulkhead. The cylinder can now be removed and replaced with a reverse procedure.

The pushrod on the brake pedal can be adjusted by slackening the locknut and screwing the rod in or out as needed.

Prior to releasing the pinch bolts holding the linkpins, the track-rod end attached to the steering arm of the stub-axle must be released. Once the split pin located in the castellated nut has been removed, the nut should be undone. A ball-joint extractor will then almost certainly be required to physically separate the joint from its tapered eye in the steering arm. Once released, the securing nuts on the pinch bolts holding the linkpins can be removed and the bolts withdrawn. The linkpins can now be tapped out an equal amount top and bottom until the link and the stub-axle are free. Always note the number of shims and their position, for reassembly. Prior to March 1960, cars have plain bushes and ten shims to each pin. After this date, the design used steel and rubber sealing rings with only eight shims of 0.020in size to each pin to adjust front wheel camber to the VW-specified negative setting.

With the steering assembly away from the trailing-arms, a measurement should be taken of the distance between the face of the upper torsion-arm eye and a straight metal edge run from the lower torsion-arm eye. This measurement should not be more than 9mm or less than 5mm on any model, or it indicates that damage has occurred to the trailing-arms. This measurement will also be used when calculating the positioning of shims in the rebuilt assembly, and it is essential that your workshop manual is referred to when selecting the correct shim positions to determine the offset of the refitted assembly. The shims are fitted at four locations on the assembly, and must be accurate.

At this point, the services of a specialist engineering shop or VW agent will be needed, as an hydraulic press and an expanding parallel reamer and guide will be required. The press is necessary to remove the linkpin bushes, which is followed by pressing out the kingpin. The kingpin bushes are not overly tight and can be drifted out, but be careful not to damage the retaining bores. Great skill is needed to fit and ream the bushes to the new pin, hence the need for specialist help at this point. This is the point where replacement stub-axles with fittings for the attachment of disc brakes need to be fitted, if they are to be used.

The reassembly sequence consists of positioning the dowelled thrust washer on the stub-axle so that it fully locates on the dowel pin. This is followed by the friction washer and cover, which similarly align to a slot in the kingpin carrier. Gently tap the

An hydraulic press is essential for pressing out the linkpin bushes and the kingpin on the earlier Beetle suspension design. Get an engineering shop to tackle this work.

Front suspension adjusters (often generically referred to as Sway-A-Way adjusters) are available for both the king and linkpin and ball-joint types of Beetle suspension, and should be fitted to both beams.

stub-axle back into the carrier and align the holes for the kingpin.

There is an interference fit of 0.02mm between the two components, so bear this in mind when fitting. A loose fit indicates that a thicker thrust washer is necessary to avoid end float, which will wear the new kingpin bushes. The new kingpin can be pressed into the assembly with the aid of an hydraulic press, and levelled off at the ends of the bushes, without being a slack fit or incurring any tight spots.

The linkpin bushes are last to go in, but their alignment is equally important to ensure the movement of grease around the parts when assembled. Only when the greaseways are lined up should the bushes be pressed in, using a padded vice and suitably-sized socket to force the bush to its alignment with the bore shoulders. At this point the units 'could' be refitted to the car by inserting the shims and the linkpins in the carrier and offering up the unit to the torsion-arms, after the seals and retainers have been fitted to the ends of the linkpins first. The lower torsion-arm will need jacking up to enable the bottom linkpin to fit, before the two are clamped with the pinch bolts. The linkpins can be rotated with a spanner on their

squared ends before tightening the bolts down fully, to take up play. This must not remove all movement or the components will be forced together too tightly, causing excessive wear.

The reason for saying that the units 'could' be refitted, is that it is possible to make further changes to the Beetle king and linkpin front suspension before bolting everything back together.

LOWERING OR RAISING KING AND LINKPIN FRONT SUSPENSION

Whether you have fitted dropped spindles or not, there is the option of lowering (or raising) the suspension by modifying the torsion-bar housings to allow the central fixing mount for the leaves to be rotated in either direction. Prior to the development of dropped spindles for the Beetle (an idea borrowed from low-riding hot rods), the most usual way to drop the front suspension of the car was to either remove torsion-leaves entirely, or to weld together the ends of each stack of leaves, and then cut away part of a number of leaves either side of the central mount. Although this achieved a lowered stance it was at the expense of ride quality due to the reduction in suspension travel, and the fact that the suspension components hit the bump-stops quicker, giving a very lumpy-feeling to the overall ride. Another option was to remove the sets of leaves, and then cut the central section of one (or occasionally both) torsion-tubes either side of the central mounting, and turn the section before welding everything back together again. With the leaves re-inserted in their new position relative to the torsion-tube assembly, and the trailing-arms re-attached to the outer ends of the leaves, the ride height of the

Avis adjusters work by using ratcheted plates to move the central torsion-leaf mounts around by increments within the torsion-bar tubes. These are ready-fitted to 'Puma' beams.

suspension was thus altered.

These methods of lowering did not allow fine adjustment necessary to achieve the exact height required and, once done, were not reversible! One of the earliest devices for adjusting the VW front suspension was the Select-A-Drop. This mounted a fixed bracket to the lower torsion-tube, and a similar bracket welded to a rotating section within the upper torsion-tube. Between the two was a large threaded bolt which, when turned, rotated the central mount and leaves within the top torsion-bar up or down. However, by twisting the one set of leaves against the other, it created a very harsh ride. Other adjusters followed, working on the same basic principle of rotating the central mount holding the torsion-leaves. The most popular torsion-bar adjusters currently are those manufactured by Sway-A-Way, although there are numerous copies.

These types of adjusters are usually welded into each torsion-tube, and they replace the fixed central mount with a rotating mount, adjusted and held in position by screw threads and locknuts. Due to the different numbers of leaves in king and linkpin and ball-joint types of suspensions, two different types are available. We will look at how to fit them in the section on ball-joint suspensions. Another type of adjuster, the 'Avis'

High performance aftermarket shock absorbers, such as these Bugpack units, are especially-made for Beetles with lowered suspension to avoid loss of ride-quality.

Modern shock absorbers, of superior design, are readily available in different lengths and for different applications. These are Toxic Shock units with urethane top mounting bushes.

adjuster, is also available from Gene Berg Enterprises. This works by welding a ratcheted plate onto the front of the torsion-tube, or tubes, and moving the central torsion-leaf mount around once the locating dimples for the mount within the tube are drilled out. The mount is then located and rotated by a matching outer ratcheted plate secured with a dogtooth bolt. We will also look at the fitting of this device in the ball-joint section, though the principle applies to both types of torsion-bar front suspensions.

Steel anti-roll bar retaining clamps are secured with a tapered clip. They are prone to rust, however, and the rubber bushes to perishing. Modern replacements include bolt-together stainless steel units with urethane bushes, or stainless steel band-types.

With both the Sway-A-Way and Avis methods, the amount of adjustment, and therefore lowering, depends upon where the adjusters are fitted to the torsion-tubes. My own preference is to fit them central to the tube so that they will give a 2 inch up or 2 inch down adjustment. This, combined with a pair of two inch dropped spindles, gives the option of setting the ride height at the front of the car at the standard height, 2 or 4 inches down. In all cases, if the front of the car is lowered more than 2 inches on adjusters, it will be necessary to fit shorter shock absorbers to prevent stock units bottoming out. Prior to the introduction of many high quality aftermarket shock absorbers, some of which offer adjustability to increase damping action, the accepted alternatives were Mini shock absorbers, which have bolt fixings at both ends for a linkpin front end, and 1968-1971 Opel Kadett units for the later ball-joint suspension.

If the thought of cutting and welding a set of torsion-tubes worries you, then there are brand-new units on the market ready fitted with either Sway-A-Way or Avis-type adjusters. The latter are known as 'Puma' beams as these were also fitted to the Brazilian VW sportscar of this name. These are stronger units, since they have not been cut and re-welded, and are, of course, brand new. Available in left or right-hand drive format (and now also in a $3^1/2$in narrowed format for owners who wish to gain extra tyre clearance within a stock fender), they are straightforward to fit.

The first step is to remove the anti-roll bar, if one is fitted. The retaining clamps on the bottom trailing-arms are held closed by clips which have a taper to them. You will need to bend up the retaining tab at the wider end, and then slide the clips off in the direction of the taper. The clamps can then be prised apart and the anti-roll bar removed. The clamps will need to be replaced by new ones upon refitting, but it is much more satisfactory to use modern bolt-through stainless steel units. Another alternative is a set of the excellent Sway-A-Way bolt-up stainless steel band-type clamps which, when used in conjunction with Spectra Dynamics Deflex polyurethane bushes to replace the weaker VW rubber bushes, give a very secure and long-lasting mounting. These polyurethane (or 'urethane') replacement bushes will not perish or crumble, are not affected by petrol, oil or grease, and are self-lubricating. They are also made in different grades for standard road use or high performance racing applications.

Under the front hood, the fuel tank must be removed after draining it, and this is released by removing the four retaining screws and metal tabs near each corner on all post 1960

Urethane steering coupler, torsion bar bushes and track-rod end covers are all worthwhile replacements for worn or original parts. They vastly improve the feel and performance of the Beetle front suspension.

Koni shock absorbers are adjustable for optimum performance setting. They are also fully-rebuildable.

The stock rubber bump stop 'snub' cones between the trailing arms should be replaced with much stronger urethane items. These examples are made by Sway-A-Way.

tanks. With the flexible fuel line disconnected from the metal pipe above the central chassis tunnel, the tank can then be withdrawn. In the aperture left by the fuel tank, you will see two hex-screws which secure the bodyshell to mounts on the top torsion-tube, and these must be removed. Rubber mounts that sits between the bodyshell and the torsion-bar mountings must not be lost during the removal and refitting of the front suspension, as these help prevent road noise and vibration being transmitted into the car. The coupling for the steering column then needs to be disconnected, and this can be done by removing the through-bolts that connect the two steering spiders (one mounted to the splined end section of the steering column, the other to the splined worm shaft of the steering gearbox) which locate the flexible rubber coupling sandwiched between them. Upon replacement, this coupling should be replaced by one made of urethane, or a superior grade rubber, as the original rubber units are prone to perishing and cracking, which affects the feel of the steering. If you wish to reduce the overall weight of the front suspension prior to removing

it from the car, the front shock absorbers, steering gearbox and trailing-arms can all be removed first.

Starting with the shock absorbers, firstly bend back the retaining plates (if fitted) on the top retaining bolts, and soak these and the lower retaining nuts in a releasing fluid to ease their movement. Once undone, the units (which on all post-1951 Beetles are a non-adjustable, double-acting telescopic type of 90mm stroke) can be removed. During replacement these can be exchanged for more modern units of superior design, such as those from Bugpack, Bilstein, KYB, Koni, Spax or Toxic Shock. Shock absorbers work by damping suspension bump and rebound, channelling fluid through various valves to convert mechanical energy into heat, which is then dissipated into the air. Uprated shock absorbers come in many different designs, but are all designed

to increase this damping function, and to help you get the best handling from your vehicle. Koni units, for example, are adjustable, allowing you to optimise the setting for rebound damping. They also have the advantage of being re-buildable in future years.

Spax units are also fully adjustable, and can be fine-tuned whilst still fitted to the car. KYB dampers are gas-filled, and designed to work especially with lowered front suspensions where bottoming-out of the stock units would quickly lead to failure. They are non-adjustable units, but do help correct cornering roll and pitching of a Beetle on the road. Each design has its own merits, and price tag, so consult suppliers for the full specification of their products before deciding on one that will be right for your car.

With the shock absorbers removed, the trailing-arms can be released. These attach to the torsion-bars by hex-head grub-screws and an outer locknut. Be sure to clear out the hex heads so the correctly sized Allen key sits in properly, otherwise you'll round out the hex head. Once the screw and locknut are removed, the trailing-arm can be withdrawn. Once all four trailing-arms are withdrawn, you will also be able to access the

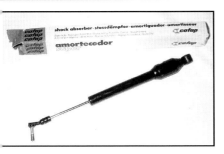

The range of replacement steering dampers is limited, but the Cofap unit is fine for all but the most strenuous off-road race use. Chromed units are also available.

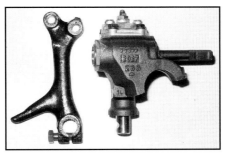

Replacing a steering gearbox, once it has reached the furthest extent of its adjustment, is easy. The unit simply clamps to the top torsion-bar tube.

rubber bump-stop mounted between the trailing-arms. This is normally cracked and ineffective on older cars, and can be replaced by either a new rubber cone, or a high performance urethane replacement. If the front suspension is to be lowered by 4 inches with adjusters, then the whole bump-stop arm should be repositioned further up the side plate, although some owners dispense with them altogether and allow the shock absorber to provide the stop. This is not recommended, as the bump-stops are important to limit the upward travel of the suspension, and snub-cones are somewhat cheaper to replace than shock absorbers.

The steering gearbox

Moving to the steering gearbox, this will still have the two track-rods attached, together with the steering damper – except on very early cars where one was not fitted (VW introduced this to all post-1960 Beetles to cure front end shimmy). The steering damper - which is a double-acting shock absorber serving to alleviate road shocks and vibration transmitted through the steering - can easily be removed by releasing the lock-plate and securing bolt on the front suspension bracket, and the retaining nut attaching the threaded

pin end to the track-rod end itself. A replacement steering damper should always be fitted upon rebuilding, although the choice of units is limited to either stock or chromed items such as those made by Cofap, or race-quality designs such as Bilstein. The latter are no longer readily available and are, of course, more expensive, but are worth sourcing if you are planning on keeping the car for several years. The track-rod ball-jointed ends are then released from the steering drop-arm by withdrawing the split pin retaining the castellated nut on each end, and undoing the nuts. A ball-joint separator may be required to force the ball-joint pins from their retaining eyes. All track-rod ends should be examined for wear and, ideally, replaced prior to refitting. We will cover this in the section on ball-joint front suspensions. At the very least any damaged seals should be replaced so they don't run dry of lubricating grease. They are secured by a tight metal band at the wider end, and can be replaced by standard VW rubber items, or the longer-lasting urethane items supplied by Bugpack.

The steering gearbox position should be marked on the upper tube, though all but the earliest models had positional marking pins welded to the top tube to prevent the box rotating.

The lock plate tabs covering the bolt heads securing the clamp can now be bent back, and the bolts removed thus releasing the box from the torsion-tube. Up until August 1961, the steering gearbox used a worm shaft running in ball-bearings, meshing with a bronze half-nut or sector which is self-aligning in a spherical seating in the rocker arm at the top of the drop-arm shaft. These units can be rebuilt if steering play is excessive, though parts are not the easiest to source. Later units use a worm and roller design, where the earlier sector is replaced by a roller mounted on a needle-bearing carried by the rocker arm. The roller engages the steering worm, giving an almost frictionless response to any movement. Although backlash between the roller and the worm can be adjusted by means of a screw, once the finite limit of adjustment has been reached, the gearbox cannot be rebuilt, and has to be exchanged.

Torsion-bars

To release the torsion-bar axle assembly from the chassis frame-head, firstly soak the four retaining bolts with releasing fluid overnight. This cannot be over-emphasised, as the years of road use will almost certainly have made the bolts seize, and snapping one off in the frame-head will cause additional work drilling out the remains, and re-tapping the thread. The bolt heads may also have a lockplate covering them, and this should be removed, prior to winding the bolts out. Remember that, as the bolts are extracted, there is nothing else holding the axle assembly in position, and it must be supported. Once out of the car, the position of the torsion-bar leaves should be noted as they take a 'set' with age and should be re-inserted in the same tube with the same orientation. The two central

The torsion-tube outer bearings are of Micarta or needle roller design. These can be exchanged for superior quality self-lubricating urethane bushes, which just push in.

grub-screws and locknuts which hold the leaves in place can then be released.

Once the torsion-leaves are removed, the torsion beam assembly can be prepared for modification with adjusters, or a completely new beam can be fitted. If you decide to use a new beam, whether fitted with adjusters or not, remember that most come fitted with the steering stop positioned for a left-hand-drive vehicle. For a right-hand-drive application, the steering stop from the old beam will need to be cut off and welded on to the new beam. If you do not have access to welding gear, then farm this part of the operation out to a professional.

Most replacement torsion-tube assemblies also come with the stock needle-bearings and rubber seals at each end of the torsion-tubes. Replacing these with urethane bushes will give a long-lasting and self-lubricating method of supporting the trailing-arms in the tube. The original seals are easily prised out, but the bearings will need to be carefully knocked out. The bearings consist of an outer needle roller-bearing (Micarta bearings on early models) and an inner plain metal bushing. The problem here is to remove the bearings without damaging

the torsion-tubes. The best solution is to use a long metal dowel to 'drift' the bearings out. The dowel needs to be passed through the torsion-tube (and through the torsion-bar centre fixing block, and inner bearings) and rested against the inner edge of the outer bearing. Tap the dowel with a hammer to drift the bearing out, remembering to work around the edges of the bearing so as not to skew it in the torsion-tube. The new urethane bushes are then simply pushed in, though remember to apply a light coat of white grease to them before fitting. This will give you a virtually maintenance-free solution to the problem of worn-bearings.

Replacing the laminated torsion-leaves in the new or modified torsion-tubes comes next, and it takes practice to feed the stack of leaves through the central mounting block. It is necessary to grease the leaves anyway, and this helps hold them together in position whilst locating them through the block. Always use new grub-screws to secure the leaves in place, to avoid the difficulties of the hex-heads wearing the next time you come to remove them. If the front end of the car is due

Castor shims sit behind the lower torsion-bar tube to correct the suspension geometry of a lowered Beetle and provide straight-line stability. These are Gene Berg items.

to be lowered by adjusters fitted to the beam, you will also need to correct the front suspension geometry. The castor angle – which is the angle of deviation from a vertical line drawn through the kingpin when viewed from the side (or between the upper and lower ball-joints on the later suspensions) - is just over two degrees on the axle beam of an unmodified Beetle. This equates to just over four degrees of kingpin inclination (the kingpin angle compared to vertical when viewed from the front of the vehicle). The castor angle, kingpin inclination and wheel camber all affect the steering, road-holding and cornering ability of your Beetle. Lack of castor angle, especially, results in reduced steering wheel self-centring after passing through a sharp bend, and a tendency for the vehicle to wander over uneven surfaces and in crosswinds. It also causes the Beetle to steer too quickly.

VW noted this problem early on, and produced curved blocks known as castor shims to sit behind the lower torsion-tube to correct any factory misalignment problems on the front suspension. Drag racers have also adopted these shims as a way of correcting (or even increasing, by using more than one shim at each mounting point) the castor angle to cure their cars' straight-line nervousness on the strip. They are supplied by Gene Berg Enterprises, and others, and are easy to fit. They simply slip behind the lower torsion-tube against the chassis frame-head and are sandwiched in place as the suspension is bolted up using longer-than-stock high-tensile bolts. The top bolts can remain original, as the shims are only used on the lower tube.

Once the trailing-arms are back in position, the front anti-roll bar (or stabilizer/sway bar) can be refitted, or one added if not originally fitted to the

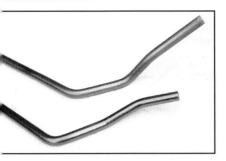

Large diameter front anti-roll bars are available for cars that will see competition action or off-road use. Such bars come with urethane bushes, and are designed for standard and lowered suspensions.

car, although all post-1959 Beetles came with them. An anti-roll bar can be thought of as a form of torsion-bar spring. When the car is in straight-line motion, both wheels of a pair move in the same direction and the bar is inoperative and has no effect. However, if one wheel moves up much more than the other, for example during cornering, the bar is twisted and resists this movement. The bar thus counteracts and/or influences the effects of weight transference on the vehicle whilst cornering, and helps control this lateral weight transference and reduce under- or oversteer.

Owners of buggies, or cars that may see competition action, can fit larger diameter anti-roll bars to aid handling, and these are available in different sizes starting at 3/4in, and fit every type of VW Beetle front suspension. They also come in different styles to suit both standard and lowered suspensions, and benefit by being supplied with urethane mounting bushes. Being a thicker bar, there is a greater loading applied to the tyres, which in turn increases the understeer of the car – no bad thing when the Beetle is known for its oversteer characteristics.

Remember to only use a bigger bar at the front if also modifying the

back end with an anti-roll bar or camber compensator. The usual and most commonly available pairing is a 3/4in bar at the front, with a 5/8in bar at the rear (for IRS cars) or a camber compensator (for swing-axle cars). As well as reducing body roll, which is the main reason for fitting these devices, the front to rear balance of the car's handling is maintained or even improved, making it much more neutral. The tyres will have to work harder when cornering, but the wider wheels and tyres fitted to modified vehicles will normally be quite capable in this respect.

In all circumstances, make sure your tyre pressures are even, side to side, to give optimum roadholding.

Track-rods

If the whole front suspension is to be rebuilt, then the track-rod ends should be replaced prior to refitting the track-rods themselves, but this is the point at which another problem may become apparent. Depending on the amount of lowering of the front suspension, the track-rods, which normally adopt a position parallel to the ground when at

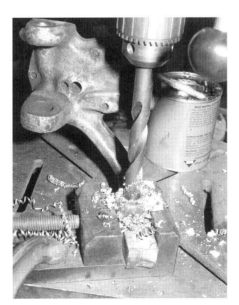

rest (and viewed from the front of the car), will now no longer be level, and will rise upwards at their outer ends where they meet the steering arm of the stub-axle. In normal movement, as the wheels rise they lift the track-rods where they fix to the steering arm. Instead of the intended straight-line movement, the track-rod ends follow an arc while operating at their altered angle and pull the steering arms closer towards the centre line of the car. This is particularly noticeable as the track-rods sit behind the wheel centre-line on the Beetle suspension. The result is toe-out, which is detrimental to the steering geometry, and ultimately gives poor handling. The greater the lowering of the suspension, the greater the upward inclination of the track-rods and the adoption of an unnaturally acute angle where they mount, and the greater the change in suspension geometry as the suspension is compressed. On anything but the smoothest roads, the steering will be deflected by bumps, and the car will become difficult to keep in a straight line.

This 'bump steer' will make the car uncomfortable to drive, as the movement is transmitted through the steering column to the steering wheel. The other problem is that, in lowering the car, the track-rod will become uncomfortably close to the bottom of the petrol tank, and may even rub on it, which is, of course, a safety hazard. The solution to these problems is to relocate the outer track-rod ends to a position below the steering arms rather than above. As the steering arms have tapered holes to accept the track-rod ends, these must be drilled out or reamed to accept special bushes

To fit 'bump-steer' bushes, the steering arm eye has to be drilled out and the new bush fitted. This allows the track-rod end to be fitted from underneath the arm.

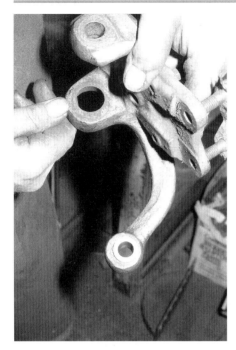

With a new bush fitted to the steering arm, it's ready to accept the track-rod end pin into the tapered eye.

Track-rod end sizes differ depending on year of manufacture. Use the chassis number to order the correct replacements for your Beetle. (Courtesy Neil Birkitt).

(available from aftermarket parts suppliers) which have tapers the other way around and thus allow the required fitting. This solution places the track-rod ends some 66mm lower than before, and closer to their pre-lowered angle.

Replacement track rods are available to substitute for bent items. These can be strengthened with a metal sleeve, welded on the outside, but this must not interfere with the adjustment of the ends.

The stub-axle is best taken to a reputable engineering shop for them to drill or ream the steering arm eye out to 17mm. If you decide to do this at home, use an accurate pillar drill and clamp everything in place. Put a piece of wood underneath the arm, ensuring it is absolutely parallel to the flat face of the arm, otherwise the hole will be off centre. Apply drill pressure evenly and work at a slow speed using plenty of cutting compound to assist the process. If you back the drill off every so often, it will allow swarf to clear. Once through, release the arm from the workbench and de-burr the hole. Carefully file each side of the flat facing-surfaces of the arm. Trial-fit the new bush, and obviously ensure that the taper fits in the correct way to allow the track-rod end to mount from underneath the steering arm. The bushes are an interference fit and can only be accurately located with a press, but be prepared to make some fine adjustment with a file to chamfer the edges to get the correct fit. The track-rod ends will then fit into the new bushes from beneath the steering arm.

Like all moving parts, track-rod ends are subject to wear and will eventually need replacing, so this is a good point to do so. Early track-rod ends are easily identified by the presence of grease nipples requiring regular lubrication at 6000 mile intervals. All 1967 and earlier Beetles use smaller (12mm) OD ends, whilst

those from chassis no. 118 857 240 (May 1968) had larger (14mm) OD maintenance-free ends which were packed with grease and sealed at the factory. All aftermarket ends are of this style, to prevent lack of lubrication and premature failure, but the threads of the different type of ends are either M10x1 or M12x1.5, so ensure you get the correct replacement parts.

The track-rods themselves come in two lengths, the shorter one being on the right on RHD Beetles. The longer, left-hand rod provides the mount for the steering damper in the special fitted end. The track-rods themselves should always be checked for straightness, and replaced if bent. Aftermarket stock and strengthened rods are available for both sides. If the original rods are serviceable, you can strengthen these by slipping a piece of 0.050in/1.27mm wall-tubing over the rods, making sure that it won't interfere with the track-rod ends or pinch bolts. The tube can then be drilled in a couple of places and welded through the holes. This will prevent any possibility of bent track-rods in the future, which can knock the steering geometry out if a bend occurs.

Before loosening the pinch bolts and unscrewing track-rod ends from their location in the rods, however, the

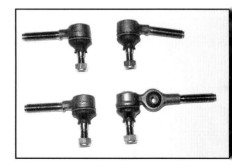

A set of new track-rod ends showing the differences in design. These must be fitted correctly to the Beetle during replacement.

position must be marked first. Use typists' correction fluid to mark the position of the track-rod end relative to the pinch bolt and mark the inboard and outboard ends of the rod. When unscrewing the old track-rod end, count the number of turns required to remove it. This way, the new end can be fitted to match the marks and thus retain the correct geometry when the rods are refitted. Note also that the short track-rod has an angled joint at its inboard end, which must not be used elsewhere.

With all four track-rod ends replaced, install the rods to the joints with the left-hand threads on the left-hand side of the car and the correct ends affixed to the steering box drop-arm. At the end of your suspension assembly, remember to have the tracking adjusted by a garage or tyre-shop with the correct equipment. The Beetle's front wheels should toe-in slightly when stationary. When moving, the rolling resistance will take up the play in the steering gear and suspension and bring the wheels parallel. Only when cornering should the wheels toe-out.

Adjustment of the track-rods is made by backing-off the pinch bolts and rotating each of the rods an equal number of turns in the same direction.

If you are fitting dropped disc brake spindles to the king and linkpin front suspension, they must now be located via the linkpins to the trailing-arms and bolted up, once the correct shims have been installed. With the track-rods fitted, and the new disc brake components installed (including calipers, discs, bearings, seals and flexible brake pipes) the whole front end must be realigned or you could end up with a low, but ill-handling Beetle. There are many different options on the actual discs which are applicable to both early and late front

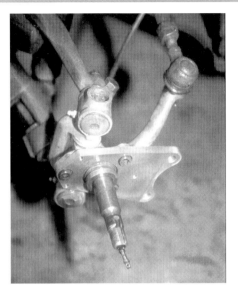

The Custom and Speed Parts disc brake system uses a caliper bracket that attaches to the stub axle, and provides the mounting for the ATE calipers. (Courtesy CSP).

suspensions, and the section on the ball-joint front suspension should be referred to when deciding on options for your car.

CUSTOM AND SPEED PARTS DISC BRAKE SYSTEM

We'll now look at the fitting of the German-made Custom and Speed Parts' disc brake system which, whilst also being available for the ball-joint suspensions, is ideally suited to the king and linkpin cars as it uses the early five-stud 205mm wheel mountings. This system uses a bracket mounted to the stub-axle and only increases the track of the vehicle on early cars by 12mm each side. The calipers and wheel bearings are used from mass-produced modern cars, thus avoiding problems with spare parts. The high-quality alloy hubs and the brake caliper brackets are CNC-machined from 1.2841 steel for the best possible accuracy and fit. The

The Custom and Speed Parts brake discs measure 280 x 10mm, and make a substantial improvement in front-end stopping power. They only increase the track each side of the Beetle by 12mm.

brake discs are manufactured from ductile iron by a large German brake manufacturer, and measure 280x10mm. The calipers are manufactured by ATE and are of the single-piston or 'floating' type where, as the name suggests, the caliper floats or slides to exert equal pressure to both pads when actuated by the hydraulic fluid in the braking system. The piston diameter is 48mm.

The system must use the brake fluid reservoir with two separate chambers and larger diameter supply pipes, as found in later Beetles. This will need to be mounted in a holder on the side wall of the luggage compartment where it will feed the new tandem brake master-cylinder that will have to be fitted for this (or any) disc conversion.

If the original brake backplates and pipes are still attached to the car, these have to be removed, and the stub-axle cleaned of any dirt or grease prior to fitting the caliper bracket with the bolts supplied, which are then torqued to the specified 54ft/lbs. The stainless steel dust cover is then fitted, which helps direct cool air to the disc and keeps dirt away from the precision

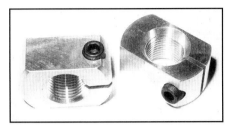

Racing-style aluminium clamp nuts replace the two 27mm nuts on the front hub of a king and linkpin Beetle, and follow the design of those used on later cars.

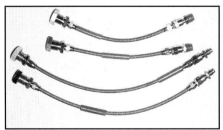

Aircraft-quality, stainless steel braided flexible brake lines. Because they resist expansion, they give increased performance, and they look good too! These can be made in lengths to suit your requirements.

surfaces. Always trial-fit the bearings 'dry' onto the stub-axle prior to fitting them to the hub and disc assembly. This is especially important if you have used aftermarket stub-axles. If all the parts fit without problems, then the inner and outer bearings can be fitted to the discs and packed with fresh grease prior to adding the rear seals. The assembled hubs, which come ready-fitted with wheel studs, can then be slipped onto the stub-axles and are followed by the two large 27mm nuts and lock washers which have to be adjusted up against the bearings. A more modern alternative is to replace these fittings with racing-style aluminium clamp nuts which, like later Beetle items, allow adjustments to the bearing float by rotating the clamp with an open-ended spanner before being locked with an Allen key. Before installing the caliper and pads, ensure that there is no oil or grease on the brake disc. The calipers are fitted with the brake bleed-screws pointing upwards, and are bolted to the brackets at a torque of 58ft/lbs. Connections to the hydraulic system are made with the new flexible brake hoses in the kit.

Remember that these flexible rubber brake pipes are designed for a car with a standard suspension. On a car that has been lowered substantially at the front, these hoses will appear slightly too long, and the loop of the pipe should not be allowed to run close to the ground. An alternative is to have braided steel hoses made to the exact length for your requirements. Besides the issue of length, these offer improved braking performance for your Beetle. Not only do they look nicer, but they are much stronger than the fabric reinforced rubber used on cheaper items, and they prevent any expansion (bulging) under pressure, which causes increased pedal travel or a 'spongy' feel as the hoses expand before the brakes are fully applied. Either way, the use of stainless steel hoses provides improved braking.

Whilst flexible hoses are necessary where movement is required in the braking system, rigid pipes are used everywhere else. Normally the rigid tubing is made from steel, but this is prone to corrosion and fracturing. It is better to install a set of copper pipes for longevity and sheer good looks. These can be bought in sets for the whole car, or you can opt to make them up yourself by using lengths of special copper pipe. This not only works out cheaper, but allows you to tailor the length of the pipe to suit your exact requirements. The copper pipes are also much easier to bend to exact shape. A brake pipe flaring tool has to be used to create the perfect flare to the end of each tube, and the brass tube nuts must be slid onto the pipe prior to creating the flare. The old pipes can be used as a pattern if you are staying with the same length pipe, so don't throw them away until you have completed your new set.

Measure the length of the old pipe and allow for any bends in it. Add to that measurement an extra 1/4in to allow for flaring. The flaring tool can create either a single or double flare on the tube, but on Beetles a single flare is all you need. Cut a piece of new copper pipe with a clean straight cut and ensure the tube at each end is straight and deburred before flaring. The flare is created by inserting the greased tube end into a special die into which a punch end is wound in. The resulting flare will form the union between the brass tube nut and the flexible hose or wheel cylinder into which it is located. All pipes should be pressure tested before use as a safety measure, and the flexible pipes can then be connected to the calipers and the whole system thoroughly purged of air.

The Custom and Speed Parts hubs do not use the original Beetle wheel bolts, but have specially manufactured nuts which can be bought separately to suit the many different types of aftermarket wheels available. For high performance Beetles, the choice of a vented or slotted wheel will also help direct cooling air to the brakes, thus aiding performance.

Porsche 356 brake parts
Another brake performance modification that is worth mentioning is the use of Porsche 356 brake parts on the king and linkpin Beetle suspension. Coming from the same drawing board as the VW, the front suspension system of the Porsche 356 is remarkably similar to the Beetle. Using a king and linkpin front

Specially-manufactured nuts, which suit many aftermarket wheel designs, are used on the wheel studs of the Custom and Speed Parts disc brake conversion kit.

The Porsche 356 shares a design ancestry with the VW Beetle, as well as some parts. The steering gearbox, front stub axles and drum or disc brakes can all be transplanted to the Beetle.

The Porsche 356 drum design features a twin-leading shoe and larger friction area for improved braking. The condition of the liner within the aluminium drum is critical: it must not be distorted.

suspension, all the parts from the linkpins outwards can be transplanted onto a Beetle as, indeed, can the much stronger Porsche worm and roller steering box. Racers in the US particularly favour the reinforced kingpin carriers which offer a larger outer-diameter stub-axle and steering arm and were a straight swap for the Beetle items, but it is the brakes that are particularly interesting when uprating the Beetle's performance. Porsche 356 drum brakes have a diameter of 280mm, and a friction area of 390 sqcm which, whilst not matching that of the VW Type 3 (Fastback/Squareback/Notchback) drum (which we will look at later), do increase the brake efficiency tremendously. Manufactured in cast aluminium with cast iron liners, the brakes are of a twin-leading shoe design. Normal Beetle brakes are of the single trailing-shoe design where one end of the leading brake shoe is mounted into an adjustable pivot and

a force is applied at the opposite end via a wheel cylinder expanded by the pressurisation of the hydraulic fluid. With the force being in the direction of the wheel rotation, the friction developed by the surface of the shoe and drum forces the one more firmly against the other, thus creating a 'self-servo' effect.

The leading shoe accounts for around 75% of the braking force. The trailing shoe, on the other hand, is forced away from the drum during braking, and thus can only account for 25% of the overall braking efficiency of the drum. The trailing shoe comes into its own during reversing when it then becomes a leading shoe.

The Porsche twin leading brake shoe assembly has two single-acting wheel cylinders per drum, each pushing its own shoe against the drum in the direction of the rotation. This, of course, increases the braking capacity tremendously. These brakes came on either the 356A model, with cooling

fins running around the circumference of the drum, or the 356B, with radial finning. Either will fit the Beetle, and this can be done by mounting the Porsche brake backplates and drums to the Beetle stub-axle, using the larger inner-diameter Porsche inner wheel bearing and bearing spacer, and the Beetle outer bearing. The Porsche design also benefits from the use of tapered roller wheel bearings which are easier to adjust and more durable, as they offer a bearing surface almost twice the size of the Beetle ball-bearing design. Alternatively, the whole setup from the Porsche, complete with kingpin carriers and stub-axles, can be transplanted onto the Beetle – which is the easier alternative.

Porsche also made a 356C model with four-wheel disc brakes, and the front pair are a straight swap onto the Beetle, provided they are complete with the steering knuckle assemblies, as they have the necessary brake caliper mounts. Unlike the drum brakes, however, the discs will not accept the early VW five-bolt wheels, using instead the smaller 130mm Porsche five-bolt pattern. This will necessitate a change of wheels, but avoids the problem of using adaptors or having to re-drill the hubs to take Porsche-style wheels.

The one deciding factor for using

Porsche 356 parts will be the price. Due to their scarcity (and age), they are not so readily available as more modern aftermarket parts. Any parts that are seen for sale should always be checked carefully to ascertain their condition, as distortion of the drums and corrosion between the aluminium drum and the liner will make them unusable.

RENEWING BRAKE SHOES, WHEEL CYLINDERS AND BEARINGS

Before we move on to the ball-joint front suspension type, let's just consider one last thing: If you wish to retain the originality of the car, but want to optimise the performance of the drum brakes, then there is no harm in simply renewing the brake shoes and wheel cylinders, and replacing the wheel bearings. With a rear-wheel-drive car like the Beetle, about 75% of the work is done by the front brakes, as the weight of the vehicle is transferred towards the front during braking. The brake bias is therefore at the front of the car, as the rear wheels would lock up during normal braking conditions if the rear brakes received too much force.

The system must, therefore, always be at its optimum performance level, and adjusted so the front to rear bias is correct. Although we will look at simply replacing stock parts, if you wish to change wheel cylinder sizes (on a dune buggy, for example, to proportion more braking to the rear wheels), keep this in mind.

The front brake shoes are secured in place on the drum backplate by retaining pins, held in position by a spring-loaded, slotted cup-washer. These are best removed with a special removal tool (though a pair of pliers can be used), turning the washer so

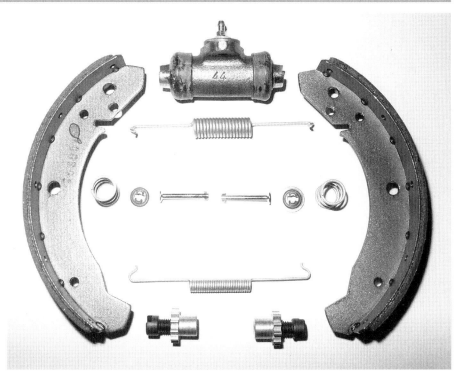

New braking components for the Beetle are readily available and are inexpensive. You should always renew brake shoes during any brake overhaul, and check wheel cylinders for leaks.

Before fitting inner and outer wheel bearings into a drum or disc, trial fit them on to the stub axle to check for fit. (Courtesy Neil Birkitt).

that the slot aligns with the head of the pin. These parts can then be removed. Spring positions should be noted before releasing them, and the shoes can then be pulled out of their locations in the front-mounted adjusters and rear-mounted wheel cylinder. To release the cylinder, the brake pipe

must be undone at the rear of the backplate, and the mounting bolt released. Soaking the bolt head with a releasing fluid first will ease its movement as they are frequently seized. Replacement is a matter of simply fitting a new cylinder to the backplate. With the exception of the very early models, all Beetles were fitted with 22mm front wheel cylinders. The new brake shoes can now be fitted by reversing this procedure.

Whilst the drum is still off, it is worth fitting new bearings, prior to final reassembly and bleeding of the brakes. The function of each of the two bearings is obviously to 'bear' the load of the wheel/hub assembly, and also to accept the side loadings and movements created by the suspension on all manner of roads. The earlier Beetles, up to 1965, use ball-bearing races, adjusted by one large 27mm

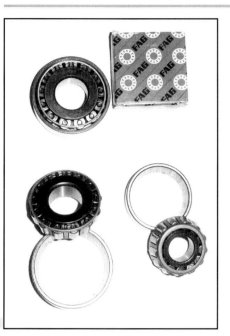

New bearings and races. The races can be knocked home into position in the drum or disc with a special fitting tool, or a suitably-sized socket resting on the edge of the race.

With the brake drum oil seal levered out, the bearing inner and outer races can de drifted out (from opposite sides of the drum) by carefully working from side to side with a metal rod.

nut, and locked by another, together with a metal washer. Thereafter they changed to the tapered-roller type which offer a greater bearing area on the rollers, and allow adjustment for wear by tightening a clamp nut and thrust washer at the end of the spindle.

Always check the diameters of the replacement bearings, whether ball-bearing or taper- roller, and trial fit them 'dry' onto the stub-axles prior to installing the races into the drum. This prevents any possibility of fitting the wrong-sized bearings to the drum.

The first thing to come out of the back of the drum is the oil seal, which will need levering out, followed by lifting out the inner bearing. The outer bearing and thrust washer will have come off with the drum when it was pulled off the spindle. Clean out the grease left inside the drum prior to removing the bearing inner and outer races. These can be pressed out if you have access to an hydraulic press, but it is quite sufficient to drift these out with a metal rod passed through the drum to rest on the inner lip of the race. By working from side to side, the race can be driven out successfully. Having cleaned the inner hub, the new bearing races need to be pressed or driven in. Either use a special tool made for this purpose, or find a suitable socket that will rest on the edge of the race and tap it in gently, again working around the race to give it an even pressure as it is driven home.

The new bearings can then be inserted into the hub, greasing them freely with fresh, high-melting-point grease. Fit a new hub seal, and put plenty of grease into the centre of the hub before refitting. The hub can then be refitted to the stub-axle, and the adjusting nut (or clamp, if you are fitting one) tightened until you feel some resistance, then back it off about

a quarter of a turn. Finally, be sure to fit the washer and second securing nut before replacing the dust cap. Check for excess play at the wheel and then, only if everything is correct, adjust the brakes.

As mentioned before, if you have rebuilt the whole or part of the front suspension, you should always have the front end alignment checked, for safety, and to prevent any possibility of uneven tyre wear.

BALL-JOINT FRONT SUSPENSION

In August 1965, a redesigned front axle assembly was introduced for the VW Beetle. The two tubes containing the torsion-leaves were spaced further apart, and the parallel linkpins were replaced by ball-joints as the method of pivoting the outer steering assembly. Tapered roller-bearings were also introduced to provide the support for the trailing-arms, and the top eye fixing of the shock absorbers were changed to a pin mounting with rubber support bushes either side of the fixing on the outward facing part of the vertical supporting towers. The separate bump-stop was also removed, as the dampers now had their own integral progressive bump-stops.

The brakes on these later Beetles were drums all round, except on the

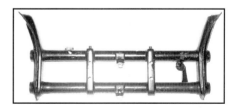

Ball-joint front suspension has noticeably different shock absorber towers which fold over at the top to provide a top mount. This is a 'Puma' beam, with ratcheted height adjusters built-in to lower or raise the front suspension.

The 1500cc Beetle used disc brakes for improved braking, and also moved to the four-bolt wheel design. These disc brake stub axles, calipers and discs can be used on any of the later ball-joint front Beetles.

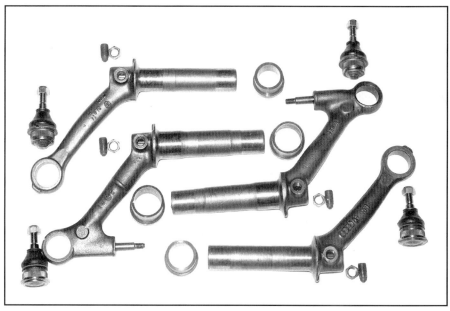

Ball-joints press-fit into the eyes of the trailing arms. These arms locate through an outer bush fitted to each end of the torsion-bar tubes, and affix to the stack of leaves with large grub screws and lock nuts. All these parts are available new.

post-1967 1500cc model and the later 1600cc-engined GT model, sold in the European market, which sported front disc brakes using the four-bolt wheel pattern. This revised bolt pattern was to follow on the 1200 and 1300 models a year later when the Beetle was extensively redesigned. US-spec. Beetles were never fitted with disc brakes, though these did appear on the more sporty Karmann Ghia models.

For the Beetle enthusiast, this revised suspension design offers two distinct advantages: parts are more commonly available and, therefore, prices are more advantageous, and the work required to upgrade to disc brakes is more straightforward and well within the capabilities of most people. We will start by performing the basic maintenance of the ball-joints in the system, and look at the various upgrades that are currently available along the way.

BALL-JOINT MAINTENANCE

The ball-joints themselves mount between the stub-axles on either side of the car and the rearward trailing torsion-arms which, in turn, attach to the torsion-bars with large grub-screws and locking-nuts. Outer steering ball-

joints attach the steering arms of the stub-axles to the track-rods on either side of the steering gearbox drop-arm,

in a manner similar to the earlier suspension design. The drum or disc brake assembly is secured to the stub-

A Sway-A-Way heavy-duty front anti-roll bar and urethane bushes replaces the stock item on this 1967 Beetle. Performance modifications have also included dropped spindles and disc brakes. (Courtesy Neil Birkitt).

FRONT SUSPENSION & BRAKES

Long-travel (or 'lowered') ball-joints are necessary on Beetles that have been lowered several inches at the front. These allow greater movement than stock items, and prevent the joints failing.

Aftermarket eccentric camber bushes allow greater negative camber at the stub-axle due to the fact that the tapered hole for the ball-joint pin is drilled further offset than stock.

axle and forms the attachment for the wheel. The outer ends of the front anti-roll bar, which runs parallel to the torsion-tubes, are secured to each lower torsion-arm.

Replacement of the ball joints may be necessary to cure excessive play in the joints, whether the change to a disc brake system is required or not. Wear beyond the .080in limit of the ball in the joint, or holes or cracks in the rubber seal of the joints means replacement is necessary. A Beetle that is to be lowered at the front will

also need to be fitted with special 'long-travel' joints to allow the radically altered steering and suspension geometry to operate properly.

Unlike the earlier king and linkpin design, which has an almost limitless angle of movement, the ball-joints have a limited movement designed to operate only at the angles prescribed by the factory, on an unmodified vehicle. By lowering the car, the joints can potentially lock up or fail altogether, as they are working at the greatest extent of their movement, just as though the stock suspension is fully compressed. Long-travel ball-joints are readily available from a number of suppliers to cure this problem, and are fitted exactly like the stock items.

The only adjustment that can be made to the factory setting of the front suspension is with the large eccentric bush sandwiched between the upper ball-joint and the stub-axle. Normally it sits with the scribed notch facing forward, and provides a factory setting with between 30 and 40 minutes (half a degree) of positive camber. That gives a good compromise between ride, handling and tyre wear, but in effect detunes the suspension, and can be a limitation for those who want to enhance the cornering capability of their cars. Minor adjustments can be made to the camber by turning this eccentric bush, but it is limited. Greater negative camber can be achieved by changing this bush to one that has the tapered hole for the ball-joint pin drilled as far offset as the conical bush will possibly allow. These aftermarket bushes decamber the front suspension slightly, so the slight positive camber becomes an equal degree of negative - but without giving an excessive static negative camber. Straight-line ability is thus not compromised but the normal excessive positive camber, which is accentuated

An ideal performance setup: CB Performance dropped spindles for disc brakes, bump-steer bushings, eccentric camber bushes and long-travel ball-joints. Just add a Beetle!

during hard cornering causing a loss of grip and excessive understeer, is corrected. Roadholding of the front of the ball-jointed Beetle is noticeably improved during cornering, as is the responsiveness of the steering, with the use of this adjustable bush.

DISMANTLING BALL-JOINT SUSPENSION AND OVERHAULING BRAKES

In order to fit an adjustable bush, change the ball-joints, or change to the better disc brake setup, you will first need to do some disassembly work. As with work on the linkpin model Beetles, loosen the wheel nuts then jack-up and secure the front of the vehicle on proper axle stands. Ensure the handbrake is on, to prevent the possibility of the car rolling backwards. With the wheels removed, the dust covers on the drum brakes can be prised off. On the nearside cover, the circlip that retains the speedometer drive also has to be removed, and the cable withdrawn from the back of the stub-axle before the cover can be removed. Using an Allen key, undo the spindle clamp under the cap and unscrew it with a spanner (remember, the left-hand or speedometer side has a left-hand thread and vice versa). Remove the tongued thrust washer and outer bearing. The brake shoes will have to be adjusted through the brake backplate (on all 1967-on Beetles) or through the drum itself (on 1966 year only Beetles) to withdraw them away from the friction surface. The drum can now be withdrawn from the stub-axle.

Attached to the brake backplate are the brake shoes and the brake cylinder, plus the return springs. The springs – which draw the brake shoes away from the drums when brake pressure is relieved - can carefully be removed with pliers. In the centre of each shoe is a retaining pin, held in position by a spring-loaded slotted cup-washer, which must be removed. With pliers or, ideally, a special brake tool, press down on the washer whilst simultaneously turning it to release the slotted head from the cup. The shoe can then be withdrawn from the brake adjuster and the brake cylinder.

If only a simple brake overhaul is required, the brake shoes, and drum (complete with new bearings fitted), could simply be renewed at this point, and the disassembly process reversed. The brake cylinder could also be changed. To do this requires the removal of the flexible brake hose and undoing the retaining bolt. The brake system would then require bleeding to remove air, once rebuilt.

To change to the superior disc brake assembly, the brake backplate must be removed from the stub-axle, once the brake hose is undone, by removing the three retaining bolts. Using a releasing fluid will help ease the process, as they will probably never have been undone since the car was built. The stub-axle is then accessible, and the two large ball-joints, together with the track-rod ball-joint are now visible.

Removing the retaining nuts from all three is relatively straightforward, with releasing fluid again proving helpful, but actual separation of the ball-joint pins from the tapered retaining eyes within the stub-axle and

steering arm is more problematic. Never hammer on the end of the ball pin thread, but use a proper ball-joint separator. A 'pickle-fork' tool may have to be used if the joint is stubborn, as this provides greater leverage between the two parts. This has the disadvantage of possible damage to the rubber seals, but this is only of concern if the joints are not being renewed. Once free from the tapered retaining eye, the top trailing-arm then has to be levered upwards to release the stub-axle from the ball pin threads. The eccentric bush may well remain in place on the top ball-joint pin, and this must be pressed off with an hydraulic press.

To replace the ball-joints, the front anti-roll bar, the shock absorbers and the trailing-arms will all have to be removed from the front suspension assembly. The reason for this is that the ball-joints are pressed into the eyes of the torsion-arms, and are knurled to ensure a tight press fit. It is impossible to replace them without an hydraulic press.

Front shock absorbers

Starting with the front shock absorbers, the upper pin mounting locates through a horizontal plate in the tower of the front beam assembly, and the top hexagon nut should be undone. If the whole piston rod turns, the hexagon on the buffer stud itself must be held with an open-ended spanner. Alternatively, the piston rod must be unscrewed from the buffer stud. With the bottom nut undone, the whole unit can be detached from the beam. The trailing-arms can be slid off

A simple rebuild of the stock brakes also improves performance, and retains originality. New drums, wheel cylinders, brake shoes, retainer pins and springs, 'star' brake adjusters, bearings, seals and flexible brake hoses are all available.

Front shock absorbers mount via an upper pin to the top plate of the front beam assembly. Spax adjustable shock absorbers (gas) allow fine-tuning of the damping rate.

the leaves in the torsion-tubes once the hexagon securing nuts and Allen-headed grub-screws are removed. All dirt must be cleaned out of the hexagon-headed end before releasing with the Allen key, or it will not locate properly and will round off the internal faces. The trailing-arms are then free to be removed, and they must be taken to a VW agent or engineering shop for the new joints to be fitted. If the torsion-arm eye is oversize, an oversize joint is available.

If the original joints were in good condition, and only the rubber dust seal requires replacement, the old one must be released by springing off the retaining metal ring and reversing the procedure with a new seal. Track-rod ends should also be checked and replaced as necessary, in exactly the same way as on the earlier type of suspension. If further changes to the

torsion-bar suspension are required, this should be considered now whilst the beam assembly is apart.

As with the king and linkpin type of suspension, you may wish to fit new trailing-arm bushes, shock absorbers, steering damper, or a urethane steering coupler. You may also wish to lower the suspension by fitting a lowering device or a replacement front beam. We will cover this area later in the chapter, but don't overlook this opportunity to make these changes.

Fitting disc brakes

The change to disc brakes offers a multitude of advantages, and it is essential to understand a bit about them. The basic principle behind the design is that a cast iron disc revolves on wheel bearings on the car's stub-axle, and a 'C- shaped' cast iron caliper is mounted straddling the disc. Inside the Beetle caliper are two opposing pistons which press the brake pads onto the surface of the disc when the system is pressurised. The disc is effectively gripped between the pads but, when pressure is let off the brake pedal, the piston seals flex sufficiently to allow the piston to retract fractionally. Unlike the drum design, there are no return springs.

Disc brakes are more effective than drums, and self-adjusting. This show-winning Beetle also has Koni adjustable shock absorbers, and a heavy-duty urethane-bushed front anti-roll bar. (Courtesy Mike Key).

Discs have the main advantage of being able to dissipate heat better, due to their exposure to the air, and this helps reduce brake fade. This condition occurs when repeated high speed braking causes the working temperature of the friction material in the brakes to be exceeded, and thus renders them ineffective – a situation more common in drums because heat is retained within the drum causing a slight expansion in the drum itself, thus leading to excessive pedal travel in order to actually stop the car.

The disc shape, too, aids cooling, as the central section which mounts the disc (via the bearings) to the stub-axle, helps allow the heat build-up to be transferred away from the friction area. The disc pads provide a clamping force, as opposed to the drum's resistance to the direction of rotation, and only make contact with a small area of the rotating disc, so cooling is greatly improved for efficient braking. Discs also stay cleaner, as the usual deposits on the braking surface are thrown off centrifugally, and do not inhibit brake performance.

The standard Beetle disc is of solid construction, 277mm in diameter and with a thickness of 9.5mm. The diameter of the pistons is 40mm, whether Girling or ATE calipers are used. It would be perfectly possible to use the stub-axles with the necessary caliper mount, the discs, backplates and calipers from a scrapped 1500 Beetle or Karmann Ghia if the parts were in a reasonable condition (the discs not scored and with a thickness greater than 8.5mm). Many early conversions to disc brakes on Beetles were done this way, and it is a good start. The stub-axle merely replaces the original drum brake unit and is located by the upper and lower ball-joints as before.

The discs themselves can, of

Standard Beetle discs are not ventilated or cross-drilled, but the disc conversion is a great starting point to improve the Beetle's braking power. (Courtesy Total VW magazine).

The standard eccentric camber bush is mounted between the ball-joint and stub-axle, with the notch facing forward to set the factory-specified suspension geometry. (Courtesy Total VW magazine).

Early Beetle disc stub-axles with correct (rear) and incorrect (front) bearing fitments. The wrong inner bearings could leave your vehicle running on outer bearings only. (Courtesy Neil Birkitt).

course, be replaced by new ones, fitted with new bearings packed with fresh grease and with new seals, but the principle is the same otherwise. Always remember that although all ball-joint Beetles use a universally-sized outer bearing of 17.45mm, the inner bearing size changed from 27mm to 29mm (OD) in May 1968. Failure to use the correct inner bearings will leave the vehicle running on the outer bearings only.

There are additional options available that you might like to consider. The first is to consider using parts available within the VW range itself. The discs originally used on the VW Type 3 (April 1971 on) or Type 4

(1969 - September 1972) range will also accept the same wheel bearings as the Beetle, and will, therefore, fit the stub-axles. Their advantage is that they are of slightly larger diameter (281mm), and are thicker (11mm). If used with the Type 3 calipers, which have a piston size of 42mm, the

braking increase will be further enhanced. As the master-cylinder size in these vehicles was the same as the Beetle (19.05mm), there is no problem with having to use a unit with a larger bore to minimise pedal travel.

Aftermarket discs that will fit the

Comparison of the standard drum brake spindle (left), a standard disc brake spindle (centre), and a 'dropped' spindle for disc brakes (right). The latter item uses a plate welded between the steering arm and the re-positioned spindle.

A disc brake conversion can be bought as a kit of new parts, including the stub-axles, calipers, discs, bearings and hoses. (Courtesy Total VW magazine).

These cross-drilled discs by Black Diamond offer better cooling and heat-dissipation, making for more efficient braking.

German-made Zimmermann cross-drilled discs, and Pagid fast road brake pads, are an excellent combination of high performance braking components. (Courtesy Volksworld magazine).

Kerscher ventilated discs provide venting to the friction area of the disc through a series of radial cooling slots. This principle is also used on Porsche 944 discs.

Replacement disc pads come in different designs for Girling or ATE calipers. Anti-squeal shims should also be changed when replacing pads.

Beetle stub-axles are also available. The most noteworthy are those manufactured in the UK by Black Diamond, or in Germany by Zimmermann. These are designed to further dissipate heat by being cross-drilled – essentially a series of holes right through the disc to allow air to circulate more freely. These discs accept standard Beetle bearings and fit in exactly the same way as normal units.

Another option is to use German-made Kerscher discs, which are of a ventilated design. Here, the disc section comprises two discs connected by a series of vanes, which provide venting through the radial cooling slots to the semi-hollow area between the two sandwiched discs. This gives a much greater flow-through of cooling air, and a larger area on which the cooling is effective, thus improving the braking as heat is dissipated more rapidly. These are probably the most effective of all aftermarket conversions, using stock Beetle bearings, and a caliper that mounts to the original Beetle bracket.

Standard Beetle calipers are mounted on a flange at the back of the stub-axle, and are held on by two high-tensile bolts and a lock-washer. The disc pads will be visible in the caliper, and should be checked every 6000 miles as routine maintenance. The friction material of the pads should not be less than 2mm thick. If the disc pads need to be changed, then the spreader springs must also be renewed and a kit of parts containing these and the pad locating pins can easily be bought. A switch to Pagid fast road pads should be considered, for increased braking power. Pads are removed from the caliper by firstly knocking the retaining pin from the caliper with a punch, and then withdrawing the spreader spring.

German-made discs from VW Discount provide cross-drilling and ventilated design in one. These discs fit stock Beetle stub-axles, and use a special bracket to mount Porsche calipers. (Courtesy Neil Birkitt).

Different makes or years of calipers use different arrangements, so always check part numbers when buying replacement parts. When withdrawing the old pads from the caliper, always save the piston alignment (anti-squeal) shims between the back of the pads and the pistons, and note their position for reassembly. The caliper can be carefully cleaned with a solvent such as methylated spirits, taking care not to damage the rubber seals. When new pads are fitted, the pistons must be pushed back into the caliper housing bores to allow them to fit astride the disc. This raises two problems: firstly the brake fluid level will rise in the master-cylinder reservoir under the bonnet, and some fluid may need drawing-off. Secondly, there is the problem of how to press the pistons inwards without damaging them. It is best to use a small G-clamp and attach it around one side of the

housing and onto a small piece of wood or card on top of the piston on the inside of the unit. Careful winding down will press the piston inwards. The new pads can then be fitted.

If there is any doubt about the condition of the rubber dust seals

around the pistons, these must be replaced.

RENOVATING CALIPERS

At this point you may consider a full rebuild of the calipers to also replace the inner seals and the bleed screws. Full rebuild kits are available and are relatively cheap. The hard part of this operation is to remove the pistons from the caliper housings without damaging the finely machined bore surfaces. This can only be effectively achieved with the calipers removed from the vehicle and, one at a time, held in a vice to initially remove the exposed piston outer seals and retaining spring rings with a fine-bladed screwdriver. This then leaves the pistons and the inner seals themselves.

You will need to rig-up an old single-circuit master-cylinder to a mounting of some sort, so that it can be used to pump the pistons out when the flexible brake hose is connected to it. The problem is that both pistons will move when pressure is applied, meet in the centre, and move no further. The solution is to clamp a strip of steel firmly across one piston to stop any

Caliper rebuild kits are available, but the condition of your piston cylinders is critical. If excessive wear or scoring is seen, replacements will have to be sourced.

movement, and pump the system to bring the other piston 99% of the way out of its bore. Release the pressure and push the now slightly loosened piston back far enough to allow the other piston to come out completely, obviously with the steel strip reversed.

As soon as one piston is free, hydraulic pressure drops off, but the remaining piston can be pulled free with your fingers. With the pistons out, the caliper body can be unbolted and split into its two halves to make access to the cylinders easier. Remove the inner rubber sealing rings from their grooves in the cylinder with a small pick to avoid damage to the cylinder's smooth bearing faces. Check the pistons and bores for any signs of wear and corrosion. If there is any sign of severe pitting or scoring, then the caliper cannot be reused. If all is well, the pistons and cylinders can be cleaned with methylated spirits or hydraulic fluid.

Fitting the new inner rubber seal in the cylinder groove takes patience, but must be correct to avoid any misalignment so that the pistons can be squarely pushed home, having first been lubricated in clean hydraulic fluid. Make sure you get the pistons in the right position when refitting them otherwise the anti-squeal shims won't line up properly. Carefully fit the outer seals and spring rings before bolting the calipers back together.

The new pads, spreader springs, pins and bleed screws can then be added. The caliper is bolted to the stub-axle mount with the bleed screw uppermost, and the securing bolts are torqued to 29ft/lbs before the securing lock plates are bent in place around the bolt heads, to prevent any possibility of them backing out.

Aftermarket calipers

If the calipers are damaged, or the thought of reusing older parts does not appeal to you, there are other alternatives. The first is to use a pair of replacement aftermarket calipers, which are a straightforward swap in terms of their mounting. The only disadvantage, with most of these parts, is that the caliper bodies tend to be wider than a stock unit, and can cause considerable clearance problems when using aftermarket wheels. This is particularly true of the very popular EMPI-styled eight-spoke wheels. When offering up the wheel, you're looking to make sure that there is no

Aftermarket calipers are wider than stock VW items, and can give clearance problems with custom wheels, such as the popular EMPI eight-spoke design.

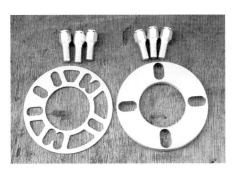

Spacers of different widths are available to help provide caliper clearance. Longer wheel bolts and locking bolts will also be necessary to secure the wheels, but be mindful of internal clearances.

contact between caliper and wheel, that the wheel fits flat against the hub, the wheel bolts pull up tight and that the taper or dish on the wheel matches the taper of the wheel bolts themselves. With the EMPI style of wheel, the wheel face has a very flat profile, and a spacer of 12mm width will need to be used behind it to clear an aftermarket caliper. Other spacer widths are available, in either 3, 6, or 9mm widths, for other applications.

When using spacers, longer wheel bolts will also be necessary, and these may also require special washers that sit between the bolt head and wheel face to ensure they seat correctly. These may come with the longer wheel bolts, but often this is not the case, so be prepared to find the right parts. Locking wheel bolts tend to have a longer shank than is suitable for use with the extra spacing of these wheels, but remember that if used on a rear drum, the threaded section can intrude into the drum and foul the brake mechanisms. This needs to be cut down to fit.

Calipers from other vehicles

Another alternative is to consider using calipers from another vehicle – the 1981-1985 model Talbot Horizon, for example. This uses Girling calipers that are physically similar to the Beetle, but with 48mm pistons. The spacing and size of the bolt holes that attach the caliper to the stub-axle are exactly the same as the Beetle units. The Talbot calipers are physically larger units than the Beetle originals, due to the increased size of the pistons, and sit slightly offset to one side of the disc itself. This latter problem can easily be corrected by the addition of thin M10x25mm washers between the caliper mount and the stub-axle itself. The disc brake backplate will need to be trimmed to fit around the larger size

Calipers from the British 1981-1985 model Talbot Horizon will fit the Beetle stub-axle, and have 48mm pistons for increased stopping power. (Courtesy Neil Birkitt).

The Talbot Horizon caliper is much larger than the equivalent Beetle unit, as can be seen here. Parts can be bought brand new, or sourced from breaker's yards. (Courtesy Neil Birkitt).

of the Talbot caliper, unless the plates are to be dispensed with. However, they are there to serve a purpose, keeping dirt away from the discs, so it is worthwhile using them with this minor modification.

The flexible brake hose is attached to the Talbot unit from a vertical position, rather than a horizontal position into the side of the caliper,

The Talbot Horizon caliper conversion can also be used on the disc-braked 1302S and 1303S Beetles.

as the case with the Beetle. The standard flexible brake hoses could be overstretched, and it is worth making the change to the stainless steel braided brake lines available from companies such as Aeroquipe or Goodridge, made to an appropriate length to give the necessary slack. Pedal travel is increased slightly with the Talbot conversion due to the larger brake pistons, but it is perfectly acceptable. The conversion can also be used to upgrade the braking power of the disc-braked 1302S and 1303S model Beetles. If nonstandard Beetle discs are used, then the diameter should be carefully checked for clearance. Using the 1971-on VW Type 3 or 1969-1972 VW Type 4 discs, for instance, increases the disc thickness to 11mm, but would foul the Talbot caliper due to their 281mm diameter. Only by machining the discs down to the Beetle diameter, could these still be used.

The Custom and Speed Parts disc brake conversion for ball-joint Beetles allows the larger ATE caliper from a British Vauxhall Cavalier to be fitted to the stub-axle, via a special bracket.

Porsche components

Perhaps the ultimate front disc setup for a high performance Beetle is to add parts from the Porsche 944, which uses huge 11in diameter, 20mm thick radially-ventilated front discs. These are the same as the 1969-1983 Porsche 911 discs, and mount to a cast alloy hub which houses the bearings and also provides the wheel stud mountings. The earlier 944 design uses a single-piston (54mm in diameter) cast-iron caliper with a sliding action to keep the pad wear even. Later 944 models used the same discs, but had the advantage of huge four-piston Brembo calipers, as used on the 911 Carrera. These calipers have four large pistons of equal size, and should not be mixed up with the rear calipers which each have a pair of medium-sized pistons and a pair of smaller pistons, thus giving the car the correct front to rear brake bias. They are also directional, as marked on the body of the caliper.

So that the conversion can be considered for either a ball-joint or

Porsche 944 ventilated disc brakes can be adapted to the Beetle suspension. CB Performance dropped spindles are recommended to mount the calipers.

A Porsche 944 disc brake assembly mounted to the Super Beetle front. The Beetle IRS rear is also ideally suited to Porsche rear brake conversion, due to its design similarity. (Courtesy Total VW magazine).

The difference between the Porsche front and rear calipers is clearly visible: fronts (right) have four large pistons of equal size; rears (left) have one medium, and one small pair of pistons.
(Courtesy Total VW magazine).

king and linkpin Beetle front suspension, the use of CB Performance dropped spindles is to be recommended, although the conversion could be adapted to work with stock spindles of different years once special caliper adaptor brackets have been fabricated. The caliper mounting surfaces would have to be milled flat and special bearing bushings fabricated, but the first method is known to work well. This conversion has been pioneered by VW performance specialists such as John Maher Racing. The machine work that is required, however, is best out-sourced to a specialist engineering shop, due to the complexity of the modifications required.

The CB Performance dropped spindle is better suited to the use of the four-piston caliper than the earlier single-piston caliper. To use the latter would require the machining down of the discs in diameter by 3mm, extra machining work on the caliper itself, and the use of bolt adaptors to accept the M10 bolts instead of the M12 size. Using the later calipers may involve extra expense in obtaining the parts initially, but the cost of adapting them is less.

The Porsche hub - the part the disc bolts to - is machined to accept an adaptor which is pressed into the hub, to allow the use of standard Beetle bearings. This is extremely important, as the inner and outer bearings are fitted closer together on the Beetle spindle, and this adaptor allows the correct spacing of the bearings within the Porsche hub. Special grease seals are also added.

To fit the late four-piston caliper to the stub-axle, and to get the caliper centralised on the disc, the upper caliper mounting holes are redrilled for M12 bolts – which are the stock-size

Porsche caliper mounting bolts - and a new bottom hole is drilled further down the spindle, once the face has been machined flat so that the pads will fit correctly into the calipers. This positions the caliper quite low on the spindle, but it does clear the disc. The use of the earlier calipers requires two new holes to be drilled instead of using the top original caliper hole. Here, the disc requires turning down in diameter so that the caliper will fit over the disc and bolt up to the spindle.

Whilst I am not specifically covering conversions for the 'Super Beetle' range (1302/1303), it is worth mentioning that owners of these vehicles can also use the Porsche 944 stub-axles, which are very similar in design to the negative-offset 1303 units from 1974 onwards. The caliper mounting flanges are larger, to accept the bigger Porsche units, the steering arm is slightly shorter, and the spindle is positioned slightly higher on the stub-axle, thus effecting a small 'dropped spindle' effect when fitted to a Beetle. Pre-1986 944 nearside stub-axles even use the same type of speedometer cable drive as the Beetle, to save further modification.

1302 and earlier 1303 models also need to have the front MacPherson struts changed for those from a VW Golf, and have the later 1303 lower track control arms fitted. All 944 stub-axles will also require the

Porsche 944 stub-axles (right) are very similar in design to the negative-offset 1303 units from 1974 onwards (left), and can be adapted to the Super Beetle. (Courtesy Total VW magazine).

Porsche ventilated disc brake and caliper mounted to the front suspension of the Super Beetle for high performance braking. (Courtesy Total VW magazine).

track-rod end to be refitted above the steering arm, rather than from beneath, to avoid interference with the front anti-roll bar. A special shim is required to allow the 15mm O/D Beetle ball-joint pin to fit into the 17mm O/D Porsche ball-joint eye in the steering arm. The beauty of using the complete stub-axle is that the

Porsche ventilated discs then slide straight on, in their original mounting positions. Owners wishing to attempt this conversion should, again, consult a specialist engineering shop to price out the detailed work required.

Using five-bolt drums
The use of Porsche 944 rear discs will be covered in the next chapter but, before we leave brakes and look at lowering the Beetle front suspension, there's one last brake conversion worth mentioning. Owners of ball-jointed Beetles who wish to create a period look for their car by using five-bolt drums, rather than four-bolt discs, have tended to opt for those drums fitted to the 1966 model Beetle, which is a one-year only model. This Beetle used a ball-joint front suspension, but ran five-bolt drums. However, it is hardly a performance modification. The best solution to this problem is to source a pair of VW Type 3 front drums with a five-bolt pattern. These can be fitted to the Beetle stub-axle once Beetle bearings are fitted and the drum backplates and internal brake parts from a 1302 or 1303 model Beetle are added.

To begin this conversion, the front drums, backing plates and stub-axles must be removed from the Beetle. These will be needed to take measurements from, so do not damage them. The same parts will be required from a scrapped 1302 or 1303. It is the condition of the backplates that is critical, so keep looking until you find a suitable pair. Alternatively, new items can still be bought from VW themselves, if all else fails. By placing the drum backplate of the 1966 or later Beetle next to that of the 1302/03, you will see that the former has a three-bolt mounting to the stub-axle, whereas the latter has a four-bolt mounting. The later unit has

to be modified to replicate the mounting system of the earlier type of backplate. Again, it is recommended that this is undertaken by a reputable engineering shop, as the measurements are critical when dealing with the car's braking system.

On the original, early, backplate, use vernier calipers to measure the bolt hole sizes and the distance of each from the hole for the stub-axle. Cut a small, thin piece of sheet metal and place it over the holes on the old three-bolt backplate. Turn the backplate over and scribe through the holes onto the piece of sheet metal, before using a centre punch to mark the holes prior to drilling. Carefully drill the three-bolt holes in the sheet metal, and de-burr all the edges. After drilling a small lead-in hole in the centre of the plate, use a small jigsaw to roughly cut the hole for the stub-axle. Bolt the steel pattern to the old backplpate, and carefully file the hole for the stub-axle to size.

Moving to the new or replacement backplate, grind off the paint around the four bolt-holes, front and back, and weld up the four holes (another good reason to go to a specialist engineering shop). Both

Early five-bolt Type 3 drums can be adapted to the later ball-joint Beetle suspension to give a period look, and better braking. You'll need modified 1302 or 1303 Beetle brake backplates and stock internals however.

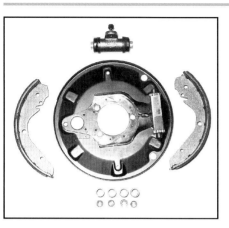

Modified backplate, larger 1302/03 wheel cylinder, and new brake shoes, springs and adjusters complete the retro-look brake upgrade.

sides of the backplate will need to be welded, ensuring the welds are good and solid. Mark the centre line of the brake cylinder location hole across the backplate, which helps locate the bolt-hole pattern. With the pattern located, mark and centre punch the bolt-holes. Pilot drill, then drill the holes out to the correct size. Once the backplate is deburred and flattened off, it can be painted ready for fitting to the original Beetle stub-axles. New 1302/03 brake shoes, wheel cylinders and adjusters can then be fitted prior to the addition of the Type 3 five-bolt drums.

RAISING OR LOWERING BALL-JOINT FRONT SUSPENSION

I've mentioned the use of adjusters to raise or lower the Beetle front suspension, so now let's see what is actually involved in fitting them. As we've seen before, the Beetle front suspension consists of the two stacks of flat torsion-bars (or springs) positioned within the two parallel tubes running horizontally and bolted to the front of the chassis. The torsion 'effect' of this type of front suspension comes into play when the trailing-arms, fitted onto the ends of the torsion-leaves, are forced upwards, thereby placing a load on the torsion-

bars themselves. The bars, being made of torsional steel, resist the loading. By moving the position of the central torsion-bar locating grub-screws on the torsion housings themselves, the setting of the suspension can be raised or lowered accordingly.

We will begin by fitting Sway-A-Way adjusters (available for either the ball-joint or king and linkpin types of suspension). Essentially, these adjust-ers replace a small section of the torsion-tube, and contain a moveable central block through which run the torsion-bars. The adjuster is moved by undoing a locknut, and then winding an adjusting socket-head bolt in or out to reposition the central mount. To prevent the suspension becoming harsh, it is always preferable to fit an adjuster into both tubes, otherwise the adjustment of one set of leaves preloads the other set.

The whole front suspension will require disassembly, which we cov-ered earlier in the chapter. As the torsion-bars themselves are removed from the housings, they should be kept together, and marked as to which side faces up, as torsional steel does take a 'set' with age. With the torsion-bars removed, work on one torsion housing at a time, and clean any paint or grease away from the area on which you are going to work. The torsion-tube should be cut to the exact size of the Sway-A-Way adjuster, using a tube cutter or a hacksaw run up against the side of a jubilee clip tightened around the housing. This will ensure that the cut is straight and level. Clean up all the rough edges after cutting, to remove filings and swarf, and any burrs which may have been

The Beetle's front suspension can be raised or lowered with the aid of adjusters. Here, the top tube is being cut around a clamp, for accuracy, prior to welding in the adjuster.

The area around the edge of the new adjuster must be clean and free from swarf, paint and grease prior to welding in the unit. The new adjuster and a section of the top tube are shown in the foreground.

caused by cutting. With a grinder, the flush edge of the cut can be bevelled slightly to allow a better weld penetra-tion when the adjuster is positioned. It is essential to now position the ad-juster where you want it to be, to allow the adjustment required. You may be looking for an adjustment up and down (to be used in conjunction with dropped spindles), or a drop from stock height downwards only, for a Cal-Look or race car look, or from stock upwards for an off-road vehicle. The internal and external parts of the adjuster are positioned and located by inserting the torsion-bars through it, and fitting the trailing-arms to the spring ends to centre the adjuster in the middle of the tube before tacking the unit onto the axle. The adjusting screw of the Sway-A-Way unit should always face downwards. Tack weld the adjuster in place first with small welds using a MIG welder, and re-check for alignment. If you are not certain of your welding ability, get a professional to help at this point. Once you are satisfied with everything, remove the torsion-bars to prevent damage to their temper, and then fully weld around the complete seam. The thick axle tubing allows for gas, MIG or arc welding at this point, and all are equally suitable.

Positioning the second adjuster is a repeat of the first, and you can ensure that both adjusters are welded in at the same angle by using a simple cardboard template measured off the first, to align the second.

With the second adjuster fully welded in, the welds can be carefully ground down for a professional look, and the beam repainted. Remember that if you go for a full 4 inch drop to the front suspension, a further problem will come to light: the steering box will need to be realigned and the steering stops repositioned to limit the travel of the steering drop-arm. The steering box will need rotating and the clamp cutouts lengthened to get it in the right position. The bracket for the steering stop will need relocating, or a home-brewed 'stop' added to the bracket, but in a lower position. The front suspension will then have to be fully reassembled.

Fitting the torsion-leaves back into the torsion housings and through the new central mounting block of the Sway-A-Way can be problematic as the leaves tend to separate. Use plenty of grease to hold them together in a stack whilst refitting, and you can use the old centre fixing to collect the leaves together as you slide them

The Sway-A-Way adjuster has a shaped central block to accept the stack of leaves, rotates by turning the adjusting screw, and is fixed in position with a locknut. A section of the original tube is shown on the left.

The adjuster is welded in around the complete seam. The total amount front suspension can be raised or lowered depends on the angle at which the adjusters are welded into the tube. Always fit them in pairs, top and bottom.

through the new block. As the suspension is rebuilt, use the opportunity to install items like urethane bushes which will improve the longevity of the suspension, and remember to have the tracking professionally checked before using the car extensively.

The other way to build an adjustable front end is to fit Avis adjusters into one or both beams – the same as Sway-A-Ways. Avis adjusters are basically notched plates: one is welded to the beam, and the other moves in relation to it. The movement, which also turns the central locating block containing the torsion-leaves, either raises or lowers the suspension. Ideally, adjusters should be fitted to both beams to prevent loading one set of torsion-leaves and not the others, and to prevent a harsh ride.

The so-called Puma beam, incidentally, is a complete front beam with similar adjusters already installed. However, the Avis adjusters from Gene Berg Enterprises can be fitted to any VW Beetle front torsion-bar assembly, and are a cheaper proposition, though there is obviously a lot more work involved.

As before, the front suspension must be disassembled, and the sets of torsion-leaves withdrawn and kept marked ready for reassembly. Front torsion-tubes have either a long vertical dimple in the centre, or a round dimple, at the point where the central mounting block is positioned. These locate the central mount, and must be removed to thus release the central mount so that it can rotate inside the torsion-tube. The central mount also has a matching dimple shape in it. The idea is to drill out the material of the tube, with as little damage to the central mount as possible.

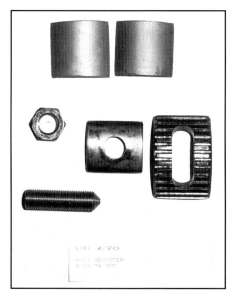

Avis adjusters work by moving the torsion leaves within their central mount, and locating them via a notched plate to a similar plate welded to the outside of the torsion-tube.

Check the grub-screw size – this should be 9/16in. Use a drill of this size to make a drilling at each end of the dimple, after first marking the positions with a centre punch. The hole should be made so that the outside of the 9/16in drill clears the ends of the dimple, leaving material between the two holes. Don't forget that there is a dimple between the top and bottom of each tube, and only ever work on one tube at a time to prevent the possibility of misaligning the front end.

Ideally, you should use a pillar drill with variable speed. Use a cutting compound and continually back the drill off to prevent excessive heat build-up, and to allow swarf to clear. You only want to make a hole in the tube and not all the way through the central collar. Grind out in between the two holes to fully remove the dimple with a small angle grinder.

You will need a suitably-sized pipe that can be inserted into the tube and which will bear on the central collar. It will be tight, but knock the collar to one side of the new slot, and clean up the slot with a round file. Because you have a slot back and front, a file is easy to manoeuvre. Slide the collar back and forth until it moves past the slot freely. Deburr any rough edges with a small file, and pick out

The outer ratchet plate must be positioned and welded to give you the movement you require. 2 inches/58mm of movement (up or down) is a good choice.

swarf from the tube centre which will have stuck in the grease.

The Avis adjuster provides about 50 degrees of rotation, which equates to around 4 inches of travel at the wheel end. Place the adjuster so that the central slot goes over the original grub-screw hole. You can position the adjuster so that the beam can be lowered 4 inches, raised 4 inches or have equal travel up or down. Aligning the set screw hole in the centre of the Avis adjuster will give you 2 inches raised and 2 inches lowered travel. If

you want to go the full 4 inches down, position the adjuster with more opening below the set screw hole – about 80% below and 20% above. To go this low, don't forget that you will need lowered shock absorbers, long-travel ball-joints, caster shims, etc. Reverse this if you want 4 inches up, and mark the position with a scribe.

To make the slot in the tube, drill 9/16in holes at the top and bottom of the scribed mark. Try and get a slight chamfer on the edge of the slot, as this aids movement of the grub-screw and central collar. Use an angle grinder to open out the slot between the two holes. Tap back the central collar to check for movement, and to ensure there are no internal burrs. Weld the adjuster units only on the sides. Attach the outer part of the adjuster with the new grub-screw and locknut, and test for movement. As you finish the welding don't forget to only work in short 1/2in lengths to avoid warpage. The two pieces of curved tubing supplied in the kit are now used to butt up to the two ends of the adjuster

The torsion-tube is modified to allow the central mount to rotate up or down. Engineering shop facilities will be required to perform the accurate drilling, cutting and alignment needed for this modification.

Components in trial position, prior to welding the central ratchet plate, and the outer shaped cover plates. As with other adjusters, fit the components in the same relationship to both tubes.

An off-the-shelf solution to front suspension adjustability is to buy the so-called 'Puma' beam. This comes ready-fitted with Avis-type adjusters and can be bolted straight on.

and cover the holes made in the tube. Weld fully around them and across the joint between the adjuster end and tube, previously unwelded. Incidentally, these additional plates are only used on the long dimpled front ends. The round dimple type do not call for such major surgery or repair, and this makes the installation much quicker and easier.

With both adjusters in, the grubscrews and original nuts which are used to locate the top moveable plate can be removed to allow the beam to be reassembled. Again there is the problem of refitting the stacks of leaves. If they present real problems, divide the stack into two equal halves, and slide the bottom half into the central collar. These go in easily. Then, remove the very top leaf before sliding the other half in, and then fit this on its own.

As before, the whole front end has to be finally assembled and refitted to the Beetle. To adjust the beam after refitting, simply jack the car up, loosen the jam nut and pull the Avis adjuster plate out of its notches. Jack the car up or down to the next notch, and retighten the nut. Puma beams are adjusted in exactly the same way.

Many of the beams available as new parts come as left-hand-drive units, so allow for the fact that the steering stops may have to be transplanted from an old right-hand-drive beam.

As you will see, there is a lot that can be done to modify the suspension and braking components on a Beetle. The most important point to consider is the ultimate use of the car. If a high performance engine is to be fitted, then disc brakes become a 'must-have' item, but do you really need the top-of-the-range Porsche items? The use of such components will require more specialised help to get them to fit your Beetle, and the cost begins to rise rapidly. Most of the modifications we have looked at can be achieved by yourself, or with the aid of an engineering shop, or welder. Most of the parts are easily available, and at affordable prices.

Let's now look at what can be done to the rear suspension and brakes.

Chapter 3
Rear suspension & brakes

In this chapter, I will look at the swing-axle rear suspension before the double-jointed Independent Rear Suspension (IRS). The swing-axle design has been used on Beetle models throughout the production history, right up to the present day. The Porsche-style IRS design, whilst providing vastly improved roadholding during cornering, only made an appearance initially on the 1968 Automatic Stick Shift (ASS) US model, before becoming generally available on all manual transmission models a year later to meet the strict vehicle safety regulations in that country. It was also available on the radically revised 1302/03 'Super Beetle' models.

In Europe, the IRS design was only available on the Super Beetles, and the post-1967 semi-automatic model (the ASS equivalent), making it more of a rarity. It is worth pointing out that both types of rear suspension are actually independent rear suspensions, with the rear wheels of both

suspension types operating independently. However, popular convention is to call the double-jointed design IRS. Also bear in mind that the post-1966 1300 and 1500 model swing-axle Beetles had a rear track increase and a

'Z-bar' fitted across the rear suspension, thus creating, in effect, a third type of rear suspension.

SWING-AXLE SUSPENSION

The swing-axle design of the rear suspension has remained in use on the Beetle for good reason: it is simple and durable, and economical to manufacture. It is also easy to understand how the system works, which is essential before we think of changing anything. The rear suspension features a pair of solid torsion-bars mounted into a large tubular housing located transversely at the rear of the floorpan. Each bar has splined ends, which fix the bars into mounts at the centre of the tube, and to the spring-plates at the outer ends. These spring-plates not only locate the

Both swing-axle and double-jointed Beetle rear suspension designs are properly called 'idependent rear suspensions,' though the latter term is more popularly used to refer to the double-jointed type.

The swing-axle design uses spring plates to connect the torsion-bars to the outer ends of the axle tubes. Drum brake internals are also visible on this show car.

Loosening the rear hub nut requires the use of a 36mm socket and a long extension bar, once the split-pin has been removed. A Torque-Meister tool also does this job. (Courtesy Robin Wager).

factory, as the wheels would then move into a slightly negative position – the tyres closer together at the top than at the bottom – when the car is accelerated or additional weight is added within the vehicle.

For general use this is acceptable, but problems come to light when the car is cornered hard and the positive camber of the outside rear wheel is increased. This situation forces the outside rear wheel to tuck under the car and the tyre tread to lose contact with the road surface. With the high roll centre of the car, together with the centrifugal force of the cornering manoeuvre, it is very easy for the rear to want to break away suddenly – a situation exacerbated by the weight distribution of the vehicle. To make a Beetle handle, the camber and toe-in measurements are critical, and we'll start by looking at the changes that can be made to keep the car from being so tail-happy.

IMPROVING HANDLING WITH SWING-AXLE SUSPENSION

The commonly accepted way of improving the handling at the rear of a swing-axle Beetle is to lower the rear suspension, de-cambering it in the process. As the name suggests, this is a process that reduces the positive camber angle of the rear wheels. Before you start the lowering process, give your Beetle a visual check on its height at the rear. Is it even, side to side, or have the torsion-bars sagged unevenly with age and hard use? It may be the case that decambering an already low Beetle will give serious ground clearance problems. The parts you need to get at are hidden behind the rear wheels, so the first job is to lift the back of the car and support it firmly on axle stands. Since the handbrake cables will also be

rigid axle tubes longitudinally, and thus the wheels, but they are the connecting member between the springing action of the torsion-bars and the motion of the wheels.

Because the axle tube is rigidly fixed at the outer end, it means that the inner end has to allow for the pivoting movement necessary when the vehicle is driven over uneven road surfaces. This is achieved by utilising a spade and socket design of universal joint at each side of the gearbox, but the net result is a high roll centre and, consequently, less desirable handling characteristics. Excessive changes in rear wheel camber (the angle of the wheels when viewed from front or rear in relation to a vertical line drawn upwards from the road surface) are experienced as the suspension moves, and toe-in is also increased. A small amount of toe-in is factory set to compensate for the outward move-ment of the wheels as the vehicle is driven forward, and this can be adjusted by moving the rigid axle tube in relation to the spring-plate, courtesy of elongated slots in the plates.

VW set the rear camber of the Beetle in a slightly positive position – that is with the tyres further apart at the top than the bottom. This is fine for the sedan as it came from the

loosened, put a block under each front wheel to stop the car rolling.

Now remove the rear wheels, then brush away any mud or loose deposits that have collected on the rear suspension components. The torsion-bars themselves are mounted inside the large tubes behind the floorpan, with their inner splines located in a block within the centre part of the tube. As the outer splines carry the steel spring-plates (trailing-arms), if the spring-plates are removed from the torsion-bars and rotated by one (or more) splines before being refitted, the angular position will be altered, thereby changing the inclina-tion of the swing-axles and thus lowering (or raising) the rear end of the car.

Lowering by about 2 inches is achieved by a one-spline movement upwards, i.e., clockwise on the off-side and anticlockwise near-side. It is worth noting that the torsion-bar has 44 splines on the outer end, and only 40 on the inner end. Moving by one outer spline will alter the angle of the spring-plate by eight degrees 10 min. and moving the bar one inner spline changes it by nine degrees. You can even alter the inner end anticlockwise by four splines and the outer by five splines to decamber the rear suspension by four degrees 50 min. (about $1/2$in lower). This was the method used by VW in the factory to correct any camber misalignment. As long as the basic principle is understood and both sides are altered the same, you can try several adjustments to your own requirements. Lowering it by more than one notch will, however, result in serious negative camber, so be warned!

With a job like this it always makes sense to first oil-soak all the 19mm nuts attaching the spring-plates to the outer ends of the axle tubes. There are three on either side (four on the equivalent semi-trailing-arm and hub carrier on the IRS type design, which we will look at in more depth

To lower the rear suspension of a swing-axle Beetle, the nuts and bolts that attach the spring-plates to the axle tubes must be undone, and the brake line clip removed (or the lines disconnected).

Torsion-bar outer covers must be removed. The outer rubber bush, which is clearly visible here, can be exchanged for a superior quality urethane item upon re-assembly.

later), and these are usually seized solid. While the oil is working, slacken the handbrake cables where they attach to the handbrake lever. Each cable is held in the mount situated on the handbrake lever (beneath the rubber handbrake boot) by a small securing nut and locknut. Also remove the brake line clips that locate the flexible brake lines to the axle shaft. They are a 'U' shape, and lever off with pressure from a strong screwdriver. By having these loose, it prevents the brake lines overstretching when the axle tube is pulled from its location in the spring-plate.

Remove the rubber bump-stops once the spring-plate bolts are withdrawn, followed by the shock absorber lower mounting bolts, and the Z-bar mountings (if fitted to your Beetle). On an IRS car, the drive shafts themselves – which carry a constant velocity joint on each end – could be removed to help reduce weight of the components and make things more manoeuvrable. The torsion-bar outer end is covered by a metal side-plate, which is held by four 14mm hex-headed bolts. Again, soak these in copious amounts of penetrating oil before even attempting to remove them, or you could shear one of the bolts off. On an IRS model, which uses longer torsion-bars to provide the car with a softer ride, the torsion-bar cover has a central hole through it to accommodate the longer length of the splined spring-plate mounting. This has a protruding end cap which will need to have a hole punched in it to pry it off. This can later be covered by a plastic cap (tow-ball covers are ideal).

Before you go any further, use a sharp chisel to mark the position of the swing-axle in relation to the spring-plate, as you will need to exactly realign the components later, to maintain the correct toe-in adjustment.

A chisel mark should be made to mark the position of the swing-axle tube in relation to the spring-plate before pulling them apart. Toe-in setting will then not be lost.

Toe-in is adjusted by fore and aft adjustment of the swing-axle on the spring-plate, with the bolts moving in elongated holes. Should you lose this setting, it will have to be reset by a specialist such as a tyre dealer with accurate measuring equipment. It is also worth using a protractor to take an accurate measurement of the angle of the spring-plate whilst it is still at rest on the metal rebound stop, before it is unloaded of tension. Assuming the chassis is absolutely level, the plate can be measured again after releasing it off the stop, and it should be at a 12 or 13 degree angle to the horizontal plane (dependant on the chassis age). Noting these details will aid reassembly later.

Now remove the cover bolts carefully and slowly, and then lever the cover plate off the rubber bush beneath it. It may take some persuad-

Self-lubricating urethane inner and outer bushes help tighten-up the feel of the rear suspension on the Beetle. They are available in different grades for fast road or race use.

The position of the torsion-bar relative to the spring-plate is marked before being disengaged from the outer splines. Refitting the plate, plus or minus the desired number of splines, raises or lowers the suspension.

ing if it has been left undisturbed for years but it will come off, as will the outer bush itself. These bushes should

always be replaced upon reassembly, and it is preferable to fit the stronger urethane type made by companies such as Sway-A-Way or Spectra Dynamics. These latter bushes are self-lubricating, but come in two grades: either Fast Road (10 points harder than rubber) or Race Spec. (15 points harder than rubber), both of which significantly 'tighten up' the feel of the Beetle, especially when used in conjunction with high performance shock absorbers and good tyres.

The 19mm bolts that hold the spring-plate can now be removed – although, even with releasing fluid, you will still find these hard to undo. Now mark the present position of the torsion-bar in relation to the spring-plate with a few drops of paint or typewriter correction fluid, or chisel marks in several places. Once all reference marks have been made and the relevant bolts removed, pull the swing-axle and hub assembly backwards carefully, so that it is clear of the spring-plate. The spring-plate will not yet have moved, as it is resting on a small step on the torsion-bar housing. The preloaded plate is under terrific stress and is extremely dangerous.

Make sure that your hands are clear of the plate when it is released from its resting place on the step. It is possible to knock the plate off the step with a soft-faced hammer, and then to lever the plate from the torsion-bar with opposed screwdrivers. However, the problem with this seemingly simple method is that the downward force may well dislodge the inner splines of the torsion-bar, leaving you with no exact reference for reassembly.

Preferable methods are to either use a trolley jack to lift the plate up and off the step (with a chain running under the jack and over the torsion-bar housing to hold the car on its supports), or spring compressors,

Spring compressors, or a trolley jack, can be used to lift the spring-plate from the step, before lowering it in a controlled and safe way.

which lift the arm from the step before lowering it in a safe and controlled way. From here on it is just a case of sliding the spring-plate from the torsion-bar without dislodging the inner end, and refitting it plus or minus the desired number of splines. It is also worth changing the inner bushes to urethane items as, again, they are far superior in terms of strength and in providing high performance handling as part of your rebuilt rear suspension.

If you decide to turn the torsion-bar one way, and the spring-plate the other, it does mean moving the bar in its inner splined block. You will not be able to see what is happening at the inner end, and it is all down to feel. Go really slowly, and gently draw the bar outwards until you feel it disengage from the inner set of splines, and then move it fractionally in the direction you wish to turn it, feeling for the next spline at the same time. Once located, push the bar home into its new position.

A couple of points worth noting about torsion-bars are these: If you do have to replace a torsion-bar entirely because the original is damaged or sagging, remember that a right-hand torsion-bar must only be used in the right-hand torsion tube, and a left-hand bar in the left-hand tube. VW very conveniently marked the bars

The torsion-bar is splined on each end to provide fine adjustment of the rear suspension. Bars are marked for left or right-hand side use, and should not be exchanged.

New torsion-bar end covers can be fitted as well as replacement urethane bushes. The cover is fitted by using longer bolts to pull the cap on, before replacing them with the originals.

Rubber bump-stop bushes can also be swapped for longer-lasting urethane items. (Courtesy Total VW magazine).

Shock absorbers come in different lengths to fit raised or lowered Beetle suspensions. Gas Spax items, designed for a Ford Escort, can be used where longer-than-stock travel is required.

with an 'R' or 'L' for this purpose. This is because a torsion-bar, once used, takes on a 'set' (or twist) with age. Using a bar the wrong way around will cause it to break prematurely. Also, if you have to replace a bar, find a good, used, item rather than a new one, as it will have the same level of wear as your other bar, and will not mismatch with it.

The reassembly process is a reverse of the disassembly procedure. Having changed both inner and outer bushes to new urethane items, the spring-plate may need some persuading to return to its position on the torsion-bar, once it has been relocated by the desired number of splines from the original position. Relocating by one outer spline will give a drop (or rise if turned the other way) of about 2 inches. A movement by four inner

splines one way, and four outer splines the other, will drop the rear by around 1¹/₂ inches. This will improve the handling considerably, but a drop of greater than these amounts will cause more problems than they may cure, as the oil within the swing-axle tubes will run down towards the gearbox and away from the rear hub bearings, causing premature bearing failure.

Once the spring-plate has been relocated back on to its step, a new torsion-bar cover can be fitted in place, but it is often awkward to line up the bolt holes for the retaining bolts. The trick is to use a pair of longer bolts, used in diametric opposition, to wind the cover back on. The two correct bolts can then be fitted,

and ultimately the two longer bolts replaced by the originals. The 19mm spring-plate/axle bolts will need to be torqued to 80lbs/ft once the toe-in markings have been realigned. With a lowered Beetle it isn't necessary to alter the standard 130mm stroke telescopic shock absorbers, as there is enough travel, although items such as the special Bugpack lowered rear oil shock absorbers are available for Beetles where the rear suspension has been radically lowered.

However, It is always worthwhile adding new shock absorbers to improve the handling of the vehicle, and there are a variety of choices. Koni and Spax make adjustable items, thus allowing you to fine-tune the quality of the ride at the rear of the Beetle. Gas pressurised Bilsteins are a useful addition for an off-road vehicle such as a buggy, and for those who may wish to raise (rather than lower) their cars, such as for off-roading, then use longer units such as those from a late Ford Escort. The alternatives are height-adjust units using air pumped up by a small compressor, but these are expensive and are for more specialist use.

There is another variation on the theme for those who wish to lower the rear end of their Beetle to benefit from improved handling due to reduced ride height, but wish to retain standard ride quality and suspension travel. Recently introduced in the UK by Red 9 Design are lowered spring-plates, which are plates with a cranked section that alters the relative position of the torsion-bar to the swing-axle. They come in fitments for swing-axle or IRS Beetles to lower the back by either 1, 1½ or 2 inches. They are fitted by simply exchanging the original spring-plate with the new one, and without altering the position of the torsion-bar within its housing. Being made of laser-cut steel, they have the same strength as the original plates and they do not require the use of any other parts to enable them to fit. As before, it is worth changing the old rubber bushes for urethane items to benefit from the greater longevity and responsiveness of these parts, but

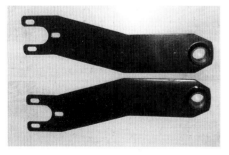

Lowered spring-plates are a new method of lowering the Beetle rear suspension, without compromising ride quality and suspension travel. (Courtesy Red 9 Design).

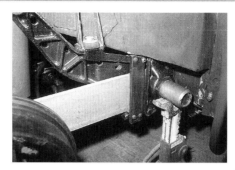

otherwise these lowered spring-plates are a bolt-on item.

If the Beetle is to be used with a high performance engine, then consideration also has to be given to keeping the spring-plates from slipping off the bottom stop under heavy acceleration. Whilst aftermarket heavy-duty spring-plates go some way towards preventing the flex which may force the plates out of position, spring-plate retainers are readily available to prevent this situation happening. These bolt around the plate to limit excessive movement. They are also easily fitted, being a simple bolt-on affair.

U-shaped brackets called 'flop-stops' are also available to prevent positive camber at the rear wheels by limiting excessive downward movement of the rear suspension under heavy acceleration. These simple devices were originally developed by drag-racers, and simply clamp to the spring-plate near the rebound stop. Both these types of limiters are readily available from aftermarket suppliers, and are a cost-effective insurance policy against problems with the Beetle rear end.

ADJUSTABLE SPRING-PLATES

Decambering the rear suspension, or fitting lowered spring-plates, does have one major disadvantage. It is simply that, once adjusted or fitted, the rear suspension cannot be adjusted without

Suspension limiting devices, including 'flop-stops' and spring-plate retainers (shown here), prevent excessive downward movement of the rear suspension during acceleration.

going through the whole procedure again. As this is a long process, this may not seem totally acceptable, especially as several readjustments may be necessary before you are entirely happy with the setting. The ideal is to have a suspension system that replicates the full adjustability of the Sway-A-Way or Avis type of front adjuster. The answer is adjustable spring-plates.

These replace the stock spring-plates and incorporate a threaded adjuster screw which enables the rear ride-height to be raised or lowered at the turn of a ratchet. These types of adjuster are more correctly known as 'outboard' adjusters, as they are fitted at the outer end of the torsion-bars.

In the US, 'inboard' adjusters are also available, but these are for specialist race use, and are complex to fit as they replace the centre section of the torsion-bar housing to allow preload adjustment of both torsion-bars. We'll concentrate on the first type, made by Sway-A-Way, and available for both swing-axle or IRS type suspensions.

The plates allow adjustability of up to 20 degrees, and are made of 0.250in–thick HD spring-plate. They also come with the same elongated toe-in adjusting holes as found on standard spring-plates, and are a straightforward swap. They are not the cheapest of items, but give an instant answer to those who wish to regularly change the ride-height of their vehicle for different purposes.

The reason for all these adjustments is to make the rear of the Beetle handle better. VW attempted to cure some of the worst excesses of the

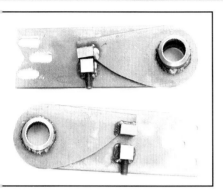

Adjustable spring-plates allow you to reset the suspension without disassembling the spring-plates from the torsion-bars and axle tubes or IRS A-arms.

The Sway-A-Way camber compensator is similar to the original EMPI design. It mounts beneath the gearbox, with a transverse, urethane-bushed, axle support bar.

Sway-A-Way urethane components include the two torsion-bar spring-plate bushes which provide high compression-bearing capability for a high performance Beetle rear suspension.

swing-axle suspension handling by the addition of a 'Z-bar' equalizer spring to assist the action of the rear torsion-bars. Used in conjunction with softer rear torsion-bars, the Z-bar acts as a form of camber compensator, helping to reduce rear roll stiffness and oversteer. It goes some way towards preventing the outside rear wheel moving into a dangerous positive camber during cornering, but is not ideal as the suspension has to move a certain distance before the bar begins to work.

Having seen this problem on drag-raced cars, EMPI in the US developed an aftermarket camber compensator spring kit to help limit the amount of travel by the Beetle rear

The EMPI camber compensator consists of a flat transverse leaf spring which limits the amount of travel of the swing-axle shafts, so improving roadholding.

wheels towards positive camber. The EMPI 'camber compensator' consisted essentially of a flat transverse leaf spring which mounted beneath the transmission, and attached to the two swing-axle shafts. Today, similar designs are still available, and they are easy to fit. Sway-A-Way make a kit that follows this principle, and also has the advantage of using urethane bushes for a longer life.

If the Beetle is already fitted with a Z-bar, this should be removed, along with the mounting struts. Working underneath the Beetle, the lowest two nuts on either side of the gearbox are removed, and the compensator bracket is pushed into place and the nuts refitted. The centre fixing bolt is firstly mounted in its urethane sleeve before being secured to the bar itself with two mounting bolts. Each end of the bar has a urethane mount attached to it which sits under each axle tube. The bar and mount are then lifted into position into the bracket under the gearbox, though this may require the use of a jack to fully position it before fitting the centre fixing bolt. It is a quick and easy way to endow your Beetle with better cornering ability, and the compensator also gives a slight lowering to a Beetle with a stock rear torsion-bar setting.

URETHANE BUSHES

The use of urethane components is something that I have mentioned on several occasions, and for good reason: bushes made from this specially-formulated high-resilience elastomer (commonly known as polyurethane, or just urethane for short) have exceptional mechanical properties and friction-absorbing capabilities not attainable with rubber. The bushes do not break easily when used in hard driving conditions, and they do not deteriorate or swell even when in contact with petrol, oil or grease. Used in pairs, or sets, they are a long-lasting replacement for conventional rubber bushes, and are easy to fit. A little grease or lubricating fluid is used when they are first fitted, but thereafter they are totally self-lubricating. The bushes release a microscopic amount of lubricating polymer incorporated during manufacture, which gives them their ability to absorb friction. Their high compression-bearing capability enables them to be lighter than conventional rubber bushes, whilst giving the best features of rubber, such as the elimination of vibration and noise.

The two bushes at either side of

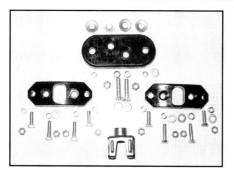

Urethane mounts for the gearbox replace the three troublesome rubber bonded to metal originals. A urethane and metal gear coupler is also available to stop sloppy gearchanges.

Urethane gearbox mounts fitted. They can also be used in conjunction with heavy-duty gearbox support cradles for ultimate strength and durability.

the spring-plate are the most obvious candidates for replacement, but there are several others, too. The VW gearbox is mounted into the fork at the rear of the chassis, and is located by three rubber and metal mounts. This trio of mounts differs slightly between the early and later cars, but they all perform the same function: to provide a flexible mounting for the transmission. They also dampen road vibration and noise and prevent it being amplified through the car's chassis. These are notorious for cracking or separating after years of hard use, and thus allowing the gearbox to move, giving tremendous judder as the vehicle is driven. If you are in any doubt as to the condition of

the gearbox mounts in your Beetle, drive the car up a steep hill and change gear from third to second. If the change is difficult, or it grates, you know that you have problems. As a matter of routine, these mounts should be changed for urethane items to prevent future problems.

Beetles up to 1973 utilise three standard mounts: two of which locate the gearbox to the ends of the frame fork in a transmission cradle, and the third mount sits at the nose-cone end of the gearbox. 1302, 1303 and later (1973 onwards) 1300 Beetles had a change in gearbox design at the front nose-cone section. There are no replacement urethane mountings for this type of gearbox nose-cone at present. The only way around this is to replace the front nose-cone with the earlier type. Changing these mounts is a fiddly job, and is best done when the engine and/or gearbox is removed from the car for other work. I have seen this job performed with the engine still attached to the transaxle, but space is so cramped in the Beetle's small engine bay that I would not advise it: the engine severely restricts the amount the unit can be moved off the frame fork. The procedure for engine removal will be found in any good workshop manual.

Once the engine has been re-moved, the two rear gearbox mounts are visible in the transmission cradle. Cleaning the area inside the bellhousing and applying penetrating oil to the retaining nuts will assist disassembly later. To remove the gearbox from the car completely, first undo the gearshift coupling. The coupler is housed in the rear part of the chassis backbone. To gain access, lift the rear seat and remove the cover plate which is held by one self-tapping screw. The rubber and metal coupling sits between the gearshift rod and the

gearbox 'hockey stick' selector.

The design of the coupling changed in the early 1960s from a circular affair, attached by two locking screws, to a flatter, wider coupling. This is attached to the hockey stick with a locking screw and safety wire, and to the shift rod by a long through-screw and side retainer. The latter mounts to the rubber sections of the coupling and, as the rubber ages, the gear-change can also become erratic. Whilst we have this mechanism apart we will also change the coupler for a metal and urethane item to give positive and smooth gear-shifting. Once this coupler has been disen-gaged from the gearbox hockey stick, the gearshift rod must be pushed slightly forward to clear the hockey stick rod.

Turning your attention to the handbrake, pull back the rubber gaiter and release the adjusting nut and locknut from each handbrake cable. Depending on the year of the Beetle, these either fit into shaped mounts on the lever itself, or to a separate plate fitted to a locating pin on the hand-brake lever. The handbrake lever can be withdrawn to ensure that the cables slide through their respective conduits without interference. The handbrake lever is located by a solid pin, which

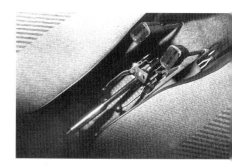

The handbrake lever is situated between the front seats. The cables are mounted through brackets, or a separate plate on top of the lever, and are held and adjusted by nuts. (Courtesy Robin Wager).

can be drifted out once the retaining circlip is prised off one end. The ratchet mechanism in the handbrake lever should be left undisturbed.

With the rear end of the car placed safely on axle stands (and not under the axle shafts or gearbox itself) the next job depends on whether the whole assembly is to be taken out, or just moved enough to replace the mounts. The former method is preferable as it allows access to all the components on the vehicle. This is why it is essential to plan the work that you require on the Beetle, as many operations can be tackled at the same time without the need to repeat the laborious work required to access the parts.

As with decambering, the mount that secures the axle shaft to the torsion spring-plate should be notched with a chisel to mark the respective positions before disassembly. The rear flexible brake hoses must be disconnected where they attach to the mounting brackets on the axle tubes – this also means the brakes will need to be bled later when the system is reconnected, to remove all air from the hydraulic brake system. The securing bolts and the lower shock absorber mounting bolts should be removed, as should the clutch cable locknut and adjusting nut (or wingnut). Underneath the car, the gearbox earth strap should be removed at the chassis end. The remaining nuts and bolts holding the transmission onto the chassis forks also hold the rubber flexible mountings. Don't lose the nuts and bolts, as some urethane kits require them. At the bellhousing end of the gearbox, remove the two rear mounting bolts that hold the transmission cradle to the rear chassis fork ends, and work the whole assembly backwards, with a trolley jack underneath to take the weight.

The solid gearbox cradle does not use flexible mountings, and allows the use of a transaxle strap. Engine and transmission noise in the car's interior is increased slightly with this setup.

The flexible mountings can be removed once the securing nuts have been undone. Clean the cradle whilst you have the chance – it is usually covered in oily muck. The three gearbox mounts can now be installed. The urethane parts all use metal insert sleeves for additional strength, but otherwise fit like stock items. The urethane will prevent most engine/transmission noise vibrating through the chassis to the car's interior, but they won't break up like the original rubber and metal units. When refitting the gearbox always ensure the unit is in position and the two large transmission cradle bolts are tightened before torquing up the mounting nuts. This prevents any distortion stress developing in the mounts. Check the nuts regularly to prevent any backing off (Loctite helps on these mounts), and use the correct torque setting on all of the nuts.

Solid mounts

The original rear flexible mounts were designed to allow the transmission some degree of movement, and urethane bushings on their own won't stop this. If you wish to locate the gearbox totally rigidly (and this will normally only be a requirement for race use) transaxle straps – or

The padded transaxle strap for the bell-housing end of the gearbox provides strength at this point, and is a bolt-on affair. A front strap can also be added for off-road use.

A high performance setup on an IRS Beetle. Porsche rear brakes, anti-roll bar and transaxle straps are all signs that this Beetle will handle and brake as well as it goes. (Courtesy Total VW magazine).

transaxle support kits, as they are also called - are the answer. These straps come in a variety of forms, from the 'padded' variety to help reduce noise, to the purely metal straps which often require brackets welded to the frame fork to act as the mountings. For road use, transaxle straps can be an overkill item, and can begin to work against you. Used in conjunction with urethane mounts, transaxle straps at both ends of the gearbox can hold it so rigid, that the internals break instead when subjected to load. For racers, the drivetrains will receive regular attention anyway, so they have a valid use in these driving conditions. Drag racers will require front and rear

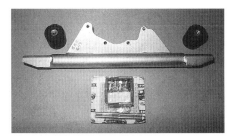

Gene Berg Enterprises' 'Super-Duty' rubber-mounted front transmission support provides total cushioned support for the Beetle gearbox nose cone.

On IRS cars, the exposed axle shafts can be fitted with these clip-on urethane sleeves for added protection and strength. These are made by Sway-A-Way.

straps, due to the rapid 'off-the-line' acceleration experienced with their cars. Off-roaders will usually only need the front mount if using solid or urethane transaxle supports, or the massive loadings and punishment involved on tight courses will begin to cause internal damage.

One compromise I have found to work well on road cars is to use a solid rear mount, which replaces the stock VW transmission cradle, and does not require any separate flexible gearbox mounts. Although it does increase the noise transmitted into the vehicle interior, this is marginal. Coupled with a solid front mount, this setup eliminates the troublesome bonded-rubber mounts, and also has fittings to allow the owner to add a further strap around the top of the gearbox bellhousing during serious race-type use. It can be removed at other times to prevent any risk of damage to the gearbox.

One other possibility, for those with deeper pockets, is to use a Gene Berg Enterprises 'Super Duty' rubber-mounted front transmission support. This attaches to the four lower studs at the base of the gearbox nose-cone for total support, but is cushioned on rubber mounts that attach to metal brackets which have to be welded to each of the frame forks, either side of the transmission. Installation is therefore not quite so straightforward, but the result, when used in conjunction with a solid rear mounting and an engine traction bar, is to hold everything solidly, and within acceptable noise limits.

The use of any of these items will be dictated by the type of driving you will be doing. For street use, urethane mounts are fine. If you do wish to retain original parts, always use brand-new mounts, and you could couple this with the addition of a traction bar at the rear of the Beetle to minimise engine movement, and thus gearbox mount wear. A traction bar is simply a sturdy steel bar hung under the engine to prevent movement as the vehicle accelerates, and these are available as aftermarket parts.

One final point about urethane before we leave the subject (for the moment) is that many of the urethane bushings designed for use on either side of the torsion-bar spring-plates are made in the US, and are used on vehicles in sunnier climes. In the UK, particularly on competition-driven vehicles, dirt and water can cause the bushings to bind up if they are not greased properly upon installation, and therefore can't move properly.

Early five-bolt Type 3 rear drums can be fitted to the Beetle, and retain the period look, whilst improving brake efficiency. Dependant on the year of the Beetle, the centre snout may need machining down to fit the shorter axles.

Always ensure that they are lubricated sufficiently when first installed, and keep the components clean to prevent any future problems.

REAR BRAKES

With the gearbox secure, we'll turn our attention to the rear brakes. One of the advantages of working on the air-cooled range of VWs is that they all follow essentially the same principles of design on major mechanical components. The basic instructions for rebuilding the Beetle rear drums are the same for virtually any year of manufacture, and for the different models, including the Type 3 – of which more later. Brake maintenance is essential for the car's safety, and your own, as well as ensuring a pass certificate at MoT time. Remember that although the brunt of the braking operation is undertaken by the front discs or drums when the brake pedal is applied (and therefore these parts wear out quicker), the rear brakes must also be in pristine condition to achieve the correct brake bias of the car, and also they are the only means of stopping the car rolling downhill when the handbrake is applied.

To prevent problems, the brakes should be regularly checked and adjusted, and any worn parts replaced. Firstly, with the car on level ground, apply the handbrake, remove the rear hubcaps, and slacken the rear wheel nuts. Then remove the split-pin fitted

Inside the Beetle rear drum, the wheel cylinder, brake shoes, adjusters, the handbrake cable and operating lever are all accessible. Early Beetle brake adjustment is through the face of the drum. On later models access is gained through the brake backplate. (Courtesy Robin Wager).

shoes are pivoted on central locating pins, and actuated by a wheel cylinder at the top of the drum, with the star-shaped adjusting nuts at the bottom. These are slotted into a central mount with small spring retainers at the base to prevent the adjusters backing off. The handbrake cable enters the drum via the backplate and attaches to a single lever pivoted at the top of the trailing shoe. The handbrake cable is held against the rear side of the backplate by a claw-shaped mount bolted to the plate. A single pushrod and two shoe return springs run horizontally between the two shoes and serve to return the shoes to a resting position when not in use. The first things to look for among the usually mucky components (caused by the dust from the brake lining material) are a leaking wheel cylinder, brake linings worn down to the rivets, and seized adjusters. Check that no oil is leaking from the bearing cover or the hub seal of the swing-axle tube. We will look at replacing this later.

If the wheel cylinder is causing problems, it must be renewed. Although rebuild kits for wheel cylinders are available, this is something of a false economy as the internal bore of the cylinder will almost certainly be worn and, therefore, the cylinder will never work as well as a new one. 1968 and later Beetles use a 17.5mm rear wheel cylinder. This can be uprated to a 19.05mm cylinder from 1958-1967 models, or even a 22.2mm front cylinder from a 1965 or later Beetle, but this will cause a rear wheel brake bias, unless work is also done on the front brakes as well. Always maintain the correct front/back ratio when the vehicle is used for street use. Removal is accomplished by releasing a nut behind the backplate. Once the cylinder is removed and renewed it means, of course, that the

nto the castellated nut at the end of the drive shaft, and turn your attention to these nuts, which are tightened to a terrific torque of 217lbs/ft. The easiest way to remove them is to apply a 36mm socket attached to a 3/4in drive bar, and levered by a 5ft length of scaffolding pipe slid over the bar. This latter 'tool' is a must for any VW owner, and will get you out of trouble with these rear nuts time and time again.

After slackening the nuts, lift the rear of the vehicle with a trolley jack and place it on axle stands before removing the wheels. Now the hand-

brake can be released and the axle nut finally removed. The brake drum will not slide off until the shoes are backed off. This is achieved by adjusting the brake shoe clearance by turning the brake (star) adjusters with an adjustment tool, or screwdriver, inserted through the backplate. These are accessed when plastic plugs are removed from the backplate, or through the front of the drum on earlier models. Careful use of a soft-faced hammer should be sufficient to tap the drums off the splines although, occasionally, a puller will be required.

Inside the drum, the two brake

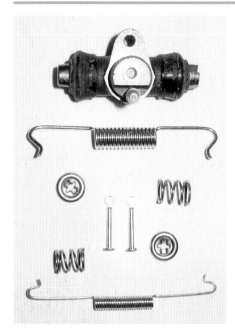

Replacement brake parts for the Beetle are readily available, and should be used to optimise rear brake performance.

Type 3 rear drums use linings which are half as wide again as stock Beetle items, and which are a bolt-on addition to the rear hubs. Late Type 3 units are composite drums, with a central hub providing the location for the actual drums.

Larger Type 3 rear drums are a worthwhile addition to the rear braking performance of the Beetle, and retain the VW heritage. The composite drum is shown here. (Courtesy Neil Birkitt).

brake system has to be bled of any air afterwards.

In most cases it is just the shoes themselves that require replacement – never try and rivet new linings onto old shoes. The shoes may have warped with heat and age and, again, it would be a false economy when good new shoes are relatively cheap. Older, riveted shoes also wasted about 2/3 of the lining material where the rivets were placed. Modern linings are now bonded to the shoe, and are made of non-hazardous organic materials mixed with synthetic resins or metal particles, to replace the dangerous asbestos-based fibres used on older designs. Modern materials also help improve the frictional properties and heat conductivity of the brake shoes.

1968 and later Beetles use shoes that are 40mm wide, and have a lining area of 56 square inches, whereas the earlier Beetles use a 30mm wide shoe

giving a lining area of only 40 square inches. The later 40mm wide rear shoes can be adapted to earlier cars by also using the 1968–on backplates, wheel cylinders and drums, although on the pre-1967 short-axle Beetles (with the narrow track), it will be necessary to machine the snout of the drum down so the axle nut will seat correctly.

Before we replace the brake shoes, I'll mention one last drum brake conversion, as it provides the optimum replacement for Beetle brakes, and is from the same VW family: that is the rear brakes from a VW Type 3 Notchback, Squareback (Variant) or Fastback. These drums give a lining area of 69 square inches using 45mm linings, (half as wide again as the early 30mm Beetle linings). The use of the rear brake assembly from a pre-1965 Type 3 model gives you the earlier five-bolt wheel pattern but, again, the snout has to be machined 0.55in when these brakes are installed on a 1967 or earlier Beetle. The later Type 3 items are known as 'composite'

brake drums, as the drums themselves are separate from the actual hubs which sit on the axle splines.

The drum is retained by two screws into the hub, and is held in place by the wheel bolts. These drums are considerably larger than the stock Beetle items (248 x 46mm as opposed to 230 x 40 mm on the later Beetles) and will greatly improve the rear end stopping power. The Type 3 has the 22.2mm wheel cylinder bore as standard. Fitting these drums to all 1968 and later Beetles, and IRS Beetles, is a bolt–on affair. It is only the shorter axles of the early Beetles that requires the Type 3 drums to be machined down, and an engineering shop would have to perform this operation for you. One final point before we look at fitting parts is that the Type 3 rear drums are the same dimensions as the front drums on the

1300cc-engined 1302 and 1303 Beetles. These use an even larger wheel cylinder, measuring 23.8mm, which is the largest VW Beetle cylinder produced, and these are directly interchangeable for even greater braking power!

Replacing brake shoes

The process for replacing shoes is much the same for all these parts, so we can look at this generically. The shoe locating springs, cup-washers and retaining pins have to be taken out first and, whilst a special tool is available for this purpose (and does make the job far easier), careful use of a pair of pliers or Mole grips will suffice. The washer has to be pushed back against the spring and turned to release it from the pin. Once both sides are out, the shoe and spring assembly can be worked out of the retaining slots in the cylinder ends and the bottom star adjusters, and the handbrake cable disengaged.

The handbrake pushrod and the two shoe return springs can be prised off the shoes, which are then free. The last thing you will need to do is release the handbrake actuating lever from one shoe. It is held by a strong horse-shoe-shaped clip mounted behind the flange of the shoe. This is nearly always damaged in the process, and will require replacement. It is a wise precaution to lay all the components out on the ground in the same layout as when assembled – it is very easy to confuse right and left shoes, and where everything fits!

Before fitting new items, brush over the inside of the backplate and adjusting nuts. If the backplate itself is to be changed to upgrade the brakes this will have to be removed by releasing the four bolts that hold on the central bearing cover. We will look at this process in greater detail later

when we cover the renewal process for the hub seals. The star adjusters can be gently tapped out of their retaining blocks and treated with a coating of copper-based grease to prevent them seizing up in the future. Don't over–grease these items as you don't want grease to find its way onto the new brake linings. Once refitted, the adjusters should turn easily against the small leaf spring located beneath.

New shoes can now be fitted in a direct reversal of the disassembly process. It is a good idea to use new washer-cups, pins and springs, and these are available as a kit for this purpose. The bolt that holds the wheel cylinder to the backplate, and the one that mounts the handbrake locating bracket can be exchanged for stainless steel items to prevent any future possibility of them rusting in. Again, use a copper-based grease to lubricate them. If the handbrake cables are to be replaced, now is the time to do the job. From their fitting within the rear brake drums, the cables pass through an outer flexible sheath into a conduit which exits at the rear of the chassis backbone, near the forks which support the gearbox. The cables run through conduits within the chassis backbone, and are routed up to the handbrake lever, where they run in slotted grooves beneath the lever itself, and are finally mounted to fixtures or a plate mounted on top of the lever.

The cables are secured by an adjustment nut and by a locknut to prevent backing off. These are undone with a spanner, whilst a screwdriver blade is inserted into the slotted end of the cable to prevent it turning. With the cable released, it is withdrawn from the rear of the chassis and replaced.

Always make sure that you obtain the correct replacement cable, as the lengths vary with the age of the car.

Later VW rear drums have plastic plugs to access the adjusting mechanisms for the brake shoes. The handbrake cable is secured with a 'claw' mounting. Changing the retaining bolt for stainless steel is a good investment for the future.

A Type 3 rear brake, fitted with a 1303 front wheel cylinder, provides the largest drum, wheel cylinder and brake shoe arrangement possible from stock VW air-cooled models. (Courtesy Neil Birkitt).

Also, always replace cables as a pair to ensure equal cable pressure is applied to each set of rear brake shoes, and that they are liberally greased when fitted.

With the handbrake ends secured to the backplate by the 'claw' mount-ing, the cable can then be attached to the pivot lever within the drum. Ensure that the assembly of brake shoes, steady springs and levers is re-seated correctly when mounted back into the drum, and tap it gently to settle it all in its new home before putting the drum back on. Finally, re-adjust the shoes via the adjusters through the backplate or drum and refit the plastic plugs. Don't forget to torque the 36mm axle nut up to the correct figure, and fit a new split pin so that the nut can't back off in use.

If you opt for the composite Type 3 drums, you will fit the centre hub onto the axle shaft after fitting the wheel cylinders and brake assembly as before. The drum itself is then mounted afterwards using the two small screws to position it to the hub, before the wheel is fitted, when the wheel bolts hold it securely. The brake shoes are then adjusted up so that the lining is felt to touch the drum inner surface, and then they are backed off about half a turn so that the friction material does not rub constantly on the revolving drum.

The car's brake system will now need to be bled to purge air from the system. Whilst the vehicle has received so much attention, it makes sense to replace any dubious brake lines. The ideal is to fit copper brake pipes to replace the rigid lines, as these are longer-lasting (and look considerably better!), and to replace the flexible hoses – which are prone to perishing and ballooning under pressure – with stainless steel flexible hoses. These are made by a number of companies, including Goodridge, and are of much higher quality for your performance Beetle.

Make sure when you do anything with the vehicle's braking system that the car's mileage is recorded so that you can adjust the brakes again in about 200 - 300 miles once the linings have bedded in. As with all braking components, ensure that you perform the same work on both sides of the car at the same time, or you will not only upset the brake balance of the car, but you will create an unsafe vehicle.

One final point to watch is that the larger Type 3 drums will increase the car's track by about an inch, so check for tyre-to-wing contact if you are planning on fitting wider wheels and tyres.

Also remember that if you do decide to use larger rear wheel cylinders, but retain the stock front items, you may find that a change of master cylinder is required. This is due to the larger capacity of the new rear cylinders, which will require more brake fluid to be displaced through the system to fully activate them. This will be noticeable as you depress the brake pedal and, if excessive pedal movement is experienced, then a change of master cylinders will have to be considered.

Beetle master cylinders come in either 17.46mm (single-circuit) or 19.05mm (dual-circuit) sizes, depending on year or model. If you have the former, then the latter can be substituted, as we have previously seen. The bore size will be cast onto the side of the cylinder. If you wish to increase from the latter size, then the pre-1966 VW bus item has a bore of 22mm, but this is a single-circuit item and loses the safety feature of having a second brake circuit.

All such changes should only be made if a problem is perceived, otherwise the extra effort required to depress the foot pedal will soon become apparent. Whilst a larger capacity cylinder may sound like a good option, as a general rule it is better to stay with a smaller cylinder to give a higher pedal ratio and greater line pressure. The exception to this is the installation of disc brakes in place of drums, where a dual-circuit master cylinder with residual pressure valve must be installed.

Also bear in mind that if you alter the bias of the braking on the car, a dual-circuit master cylinder may lose efficiency. This is simply because its very design uses two pistons in one bore operated by a common pushrod depressed by the foot pedal. The rear piston of this type of cylinder has a greater stroke than the front piston and, in normal use, pressurises the front wheel cylinders. These cylinders are the largest ones, to allow for the greater braking effect when the vehicle weight is transferred forward during braking. By swapping cylinders around, you may end up with the master cylinder over-pressurising the front brakes, and under-pressurising the rear brakes. In this scenario, the brake lines at the master cylinder would have to be switched around.

These types of changes begin to take in more specialist areas of brake theory, and it will be advisable to consult dedicated books on this subject if you are planning anything relating to drum brakes beyond the accepted conversions discussed here.

A disc brake setup at the front of your Beetle, with larger drums at the rear, or a rear disc brake setup are definitely the way to go for performance and safety. If brake bias requires altering this combination, then consider fitting a brake proportioning valve into the circuit to restore the balance.

FITTING REAR DISC BRAKES

Fitting rear disc brakes is the most desirable option of all on a Beetle. This was something that VW themselves never considered necessary during the production lifetime of the Beetle. However, the advent of much more powerful engines and better suspension setups for the car has also ensured that aftermarket parts suppliers have come to the rescue of the many owners who wish to have the braking potential to match the rest of their vehicle.

Rear disc conversions are now available from companies such as

The UK-based German Car Company sell a complete kit to fit rear disc brakes to the Beetle. The design uses a composite hub. (Courtesy Total VW magazine).

VW never fitted rear disc brakes to the Beetle, but adding them is a major consideration for those who wish to have maximum braking performance on a high performance car.

German-made Kerscher discs are of solid construction, and use a mounting bracket to locate the caliper.

VW Golf Mk 3 calipers are used in the German Car Company rear disc brake kit. This means good availability of spare parts and replacement disc pads.

Kerscher in Germany (which is a fully TUV approved system), CB Performance in the US, and the German Car

Company in the UK, the latter of which uses the calipers from the Mk 3 VW Golf for ease of sourcing spares.

Oil seals

Fitting these kits is a very straightforward operation and, like many other things we have covered already, it is best to plan this when undertaking other work. I am particularly thinking of the renewal of the rear hub oil seals, as the two operations fit together perfectly. Problems with the oil seals and washers on the rear hub of swing-axle Beetles first make their presence known by signs of oil appearing on the brake backplate (usually at the bottom edge, due to gravity). Such oil loss is serious as it could not only contaminate your brake shoe linings, but the rear wheel bearings of the swing-axle cars depend on lubrication from the gearbox oil through the axle shafts. Naturally, this must all be kept in check by good quality and well-fitting seals.

The later IRS cars do not use such a complex set of retaining seals

since they have no oil contained within axle tubes. Instead they have a four Constant Velocity joint system that we will come to later on. As with our overhaul of the rear brakes, the rear drums need to be removed, and it is preferable to completely strip the drum of all internals. If you are changing the brake backplates to accept one of the conversions already covered, or you are converting to a disc setup, then it is a pre-requisite of the conversion. At the centre of the mechanism, surrounding the protruding axle shaft, is a bearing cover affixed by four bolts. These bolts may never have been undone before and you will need to use penetrating oil on them prior to applying any torque with a socket. The bolt heads are a non-standard size (14mm), so take care not to damage them.

Once removed, the cover can carefully be prised away from the brake backplate to which it will, no doubt, have adhered by means of the paper gasket sandwiched between the two. Be prepared to mop up any escaping oil quickly. This is oil from

The central bearing cover is released to allow the brake backplate to be removed for disc brake conversion. On swing-axle models, the gearbox oil will drain from the axle tube.

The disc brake caliper mount is fitted in place of the backplate. Gaskets and seals are renewed before the bearing cover is fitted. (Courtesy Total VW magazine).

Complete installation of the new rear disc brake setup. VW Golf calipers are fitted to the new mounting bracket, and modified handbrake cable ends allow the otherwise standard new Beetle cables to be used. (Courtesy Total VW magazine).

The fitted disc brake conversion looks like a factory design. Braking improvement is noticeable on any Beetle fitted with this worthwhile modification. (Courtesy Mike Key).

the gearbox and so, once the operation is complete, check the gearbox oil level, and refill with SAE 90 grade oil. The oil plug is on the side of the gearbox.

After removing the cover, take off the outer spacer, rubber sealing ring (O-ring) and washer. Unless you need to change it, don't disturb the bearing, though you should take out the washer and clean it up. Scrape the remains of the paper gasket off the facing surfaces and turn your attention to the bearing cover. Within its recess sits an oil seal and an oil flinger. The latter is like a large washer and has to be centred on the axle shaft when refitting.

Early-model Beetles use an oil deflector and tube fitted inside the brake drum instead, but the function is the same – to prevent any oil getting from the end of the axle shaft into the brake drum. If you have this arrangement, make sure that the tube is as close to the drum as possible to prevent it fouling the brake shoes.

Cars fitted with an oil flinger also have a lug and drilled hole in the lowest edge of the bearing cover. This matches the hole in the paper gasket and allows any oil which does get past the oil seal to drain away behind the backplate. This hole should be cleaned

out with a piece of wire during rebuild, as they invariably clog up.

The old oil seal can be drifted out of the bearing cover with a suitably-sized socket, and a new one fitted with another socket, taking care to keep it square as it is knocked in. This should be lightly lubricated with oil around the edge to help ease it in, and to prevent damage. This seal also retains the oil flinger in place, so don't forget to replace it in the bearing cover before drifting in the new seal. Check the ball bearings visible at the inner end of the protruding shaft once they are dry and, if they are intact and show no visible wear, leave them and start reassembly. If the backplate is to be changed, now is the time to ease it away from the axle tube housing, and exchange it with the new plate. If a disc brake arrangement is to be fitted, then the backplate is also removed.

Fitting calipers and discs

In the case of the German Car Company or CB Performance disc brake assemblies, a special cast caliper mount is fitted in place of the backplate. A paper gasket is then added, as it would be in the case of merely rebuilding a standard drum. A

new large rubber sealing gasket is also fitted around the bearing cage. It is a fiddle, but do not twist it whilst fitting. Refit the steel washer, small sealing ring and outer spacer which is rounded on the inner face to fit the radius of the sealing ring, as the bevel on the outer surface acts as a lead when fitting the outer cover and oil seal. Again, oil the surface of the oil seal lightly and then realign and fit the bearing cover itself. The oil flinger needs to be centralised to fit over the axle shaft, and the drain hole of the cover needs to be at the bottom. Fit and re-torque the nuts to 40lb/ft. The Kerscher disc brake kit dispenses with the original bearing cover, and uses instead a cast aluminium hub seal retainer and caliper mounting in one.

A high performance Beetle, with IRS rear suspension and the Kerscher rear disc brake conversion, fitted with VW Corrado calipers. Bilstein shock absorbers, a 19mm Kerscher rear sway bar and Kunifer and steel brake lines are all excellent performance options.
(Courtesy Mike Key).

The Porsche 944 rear disc brake assembly is the ideal high performance brake upgrade for a Beetle, and is ideally suited to adaptation to the IRS models. Even the diagonal A-arms can be transplanted.
(Courtesy Total VW magazine).

This is still bolted down using the original four bolts.

On a Beetle retaining drum brakes, the build-up procedure for the brakes is as I have described previously.

For the Kerscher conversion, the rear discs are one-piece, non-ventilated units, which match up to the splines on the VW axle. The calipers mount to the cast bearing cover/adaptor, and accept the stock Beetle handbrake cables. The brake pipes also need to be connected, and the brakes bled. As with replacement of a standard drum, the axle nut must be refitted and torqued up when the car is back on its wheels. The split pin should also be refitted through the rear nut and axle to prevent anything working itself loose.

The conversions supplied by the German Car Company and CB Performance use composite type discs that, like late Type 3 drums, mount to a hub bolted to the axle shaft. The disc itself (again, non-ventilated) is located by small screws, then bolted through the disc centre flange to the hub. These conversions use handbrake cables with modified ends to attach to the Golf calipers, but are a straightforward operation to fit.

Finally, on the subject of rear disc brake conversions, comes the ventilated rear discs from a Porsche 944. We will take a closer look at this conversion in its entirety under the section on Independent Rear Suspensions, as it is ideally suited to conversion onto the later Beetles. However, the discs, which are radially ventilated and measure 289mm in diameter by 20mm thick, fit to cast steel hubs which slide onto the Beetle axle splines and are bolted up with the standard 36mm nuts. A cast alloy adapter plate carries the caliper mount and also forms part of a rear wheel bearing housing of the same dimensions as the Beetle. This allows it to be fitted to any model Beetle. This replaces the complete drum and backplate components as we have seen with the other disc brake conversions.

The problem arises on pre-1967 Beetles which have a narrow rear track, and axle shafts with shorter splines to the outer end on which the Porsche hub must fit. The options are either to change the axle shafts and wheel bearing housings to those from a pre-1968 Type 3, or those from a post-1968 Beetle. These have longer splines, but they do increase the track of the vehicle from 50.7in to 53.6in as they are longer shafts overall (27.75in as opposed to the 26.75in of the shorter axles). The longer splines at the end of the axles are the same length as those on the IRS Beetles, which are also the same as those on the Porsche 924 and 944 models, showing the common design ancestry throughout the VW and Porsche range of vehicles.

Axle gaiters

Whilst we are looking at the rear end of the swing-axle suspension, there is another maintenance item that needs taking care of before we move on: axle gaiters.

The gearbox of the swing-axle Beetle sits in the fork at the rear of the chassis, and has two axle shafts housed in tubes with the outer ends of the shafts supported in ball bearings in the rear hub assemblies. The inner ends of the shafts are flattened into 'spades' to match the fulcrum plates mounted in slots in the gearbox differential side gears. These inner ends move freely in spherical housings, which form ball-joints centring on the axle shaft universal

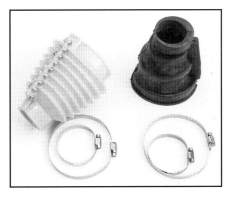

Swing-axle replacement rubber gaiters come in split form to ease fitting. Original rubber or coloured high-grade copolymer gaiters are available.

joints. Rubber gaiters (or dust sleeves) are wrapped around the inner ends of the tubes to protect against dirt and to prevent oil spillage. You can always tell if a car still has the original gaiters because they are one-piece sleeves, clamped and sealed at either end with suitably sized worm-drive (jubilee) clips. The gaiters nearly always split or crack with age and use, and consequently leak gearbox oil. This is bad news for the gearbox as it is gradually losing its oil, and the oil is unsightly on the axle tubes as it runs down towards the hubs.

These one-piece sleeves cannot be renewed without removing the bearing housing at the outer end of the axle tube. This is affixed to the outer end of the axle tube with a pressed dowel pin, and is a major operation to remove and replace successfully. To avoid this, replacement gaiters are made as 'split' items for easy fitting. In other words, the gaiter wraps around the axle tube and is held together by small nuts and bolts. Gaiters are available in normal black rubber, or high-grade copolymer which is not only stronger, but available in different colours.

In order to replace the old gaiters, set the back end of the car up on axle stands once the wheel nuts are loos-

The new gaiter is wrapped around the axle tube and held in place with a row of small nuts and bolts on the top edge. The metal clips at either end can be replaced by stainless steel items.

ened, preferably trying to keep the axle tubes as level as possible. If they swing into positive camber it tends to make the job harder, as the gaiter becomes trapped between the axle shaft and the frame fork. Remove the rear wheels for better access, and place a drip tray under the side you are working on since there will almost certainly be half a pint of old oil trapped inside which will otherwise spill everywhere.

Remove or cut off the old worm-drive clip and cut away the old gaiter. Clean the axle tube and use a little jointing compound on the mating faces of the new split sleeve. A silicone sealant such as that used for aquaria is an ideal type of compound for this job. Ensure that the split in the sleeve is faced slightly back from horizontal at the top edge. This prevents the sleeve from trying to open when the suspension is compressed, which could cause oil leaks.

With the sleeve carefully positioned around the axle tube and retaining plate on the gearbox, put the small bolts and washers through the relevant holes and fasten the corresponding nuts loosely. Do not finish tightening these until the axle is in a loaded condition with the vehicle on the ground. It is possible that the gaiter may need some adjustment if it becomes strained or twisted before fitting the new clamps. Don't overtighten the clamps or screws; the sealant should ensure that the gaiter remains oil-tight.

Transmission oil
Check that the transmission is topped up with SAE 90 hypoid oil to replace any that has been lost. The filler plug is located on the side of the gearbox and requires a large hex-headed key to undo it. As a routine, gear oil should be checked every 6000 miles

and changed at 30,000 mile intervals. The Beetle gearbox holds just under four pints unless it is newly rebuilt, in which case an extra half-pint is required. When refilling a VW gearbox, put the car up on axle stands first, and then wipe the drain plug and filler plug clean with a rag. Make sure you have a container ready before you remove the bottom drain plug!

Always remove the filler plug before undoing the drain plug – not only does it ease draining by allowing the ingress of air, but it also avoids the possible situation whereby you drain the oil only to find that the filler plug has seized in place! When refilling, it is often easier to jack the left side of the car up by itself so that it is at an angle. That way it is simpler to get all the oil in from the plastic bottle the oil normally comes in.

INDEPENDENT REAR SUSPENSION

Beetles from 1968 onwards began to utilise a different type of rear suspension, called Independent Rear Suspension (IRS), which first appeared on the Automatic Stick Shift models in the US market, and the semi–automatic in Europe. This was later adopted on all US models to meet increasingly stringent road safety regulations, but was only available in Europe on the 1302/02S and 1303/03S models. European Beetles, and current-model Beetles produced in Mexico, continue to use the simpler swing-axle design, but remains prone to adverse camber changes of the rear wheels during hard cornering, and does little to inspire driver confidence in the wet.

The IRS system still uses transverse torsion-bars, but these are of a longer length ($26^{9}/_{16}$in as opposed to the $21^{3}/_{4}$in of the swing-axle design) and lower rate to provide a softer ride.

joints to attach the axle to the gearbox via a drive shaft in the middle. The CV joints provide the means by which drive is transmitted from the gearbox to the outer stub-axle, while accommodating the angular changes during suspension movement. The axles only serve to transmit the engine power to the wheels; unlike the swing-axles they do not locate them in any way.

The geometry of the semi-trailing-arm gives only small camber change and toe-out with wheel travel, thereby providing optimum handling. This is the same system that has been used on the Porsche 911 range since 1965, and the Porsche 924 and 944 models, thus allowing us some interchangeability, as we will see later.

The CV joints are critical to the overall performance of this revised system. The standard Beetle CV joint utilises steel balls packed in grease, between an inner and outer race, or cage. As power is applied from the engine, through the gearbox, it is transmitted from one race to the other through the steel balls. The inner cage is located onto the splines of the axle at each end and abutts a shoulder on the axle shaft. The axle is free to move with a longitudinal movement in and out of the joints. This is a pre-requisite of this design as, unlike the swing-axle design, the distance between the drive flange on the gearbox and the stub-axle flange at the wheel hub changes

Rear axle-shafts of the IRS Beetle have CV joints at each end, a design which provides optimum handling since it does not allow the adverse camber changes associated with the swing-axle design.

However, the rigid axle tubes are replaced by a semi-trailing-arm design, consisting of the spring-plate and a diagonal arm mounted near the torsion tube centre to physically locate

the wheel and provide the means of pivoting the suspension during wheel travel. The drive arrangement comprises a short stub-axle at the wheel hub, and two constant velocity (CV)

Disassembled IRS Beetle axle shaft components. The metal axle-shaft locates into the inner-splined CV joints, which are held by a concave washer and circlip. Axle gaiters keep out dirt.

A special tool is required to remove the hex-headed bolts that locate the CV joint to the stub-axle. Semi-circular spreader plates spread the load as the bolts are torqued down.

High-grade coloured copolymer gaiters are ideal replacements for the stock rubber ones which may have split or perished.

with the travel of the rear suspension.

Wear in the joints usually makes its presence known by knocking noises coming from the rear end of the car under acceleration, or while cornering. Re-greasing the joints may effect a cure, albeit on a temporary basis, but it is worthwhile to change them for your own peace of mind. We'll begin by replacing standard CV joints before looking at other possibilities.

REPLACING CV JOINTS

Standard units

Having acquired the replacement joints, the first job is to jack-up the rear of the car and position it safely on axle stands. Looking at the axle shafts on each side of the gearbox you will see the joints at each end, covered by rubber gaiters, similar to those on a swing-axle Beetle. The gaiter and joint are held to the drive flange at each end by a series of hex-headed bolts torqued down on to steel semicircular spreader plates. To remove these you will need a special hex-headed spline

tool, and the job cannot be attempted without one of these. These bolts are always covered in filth and road muck and you must spend a few minutes methodically cleaning out the heads of each bolt or you will strip the delicate splined heads when pressure is applied.

With all the bolts undone from both ends, a few short sharp taps with a soft-faced hammer will release the CV joints from their resting place. Do one at a time so that the whole unit does not fall on to you or the ground. Lift the unit away and on to a bench for disassembly. Wipe the grease from the top so the securing circlip can be seen, and hold the unit in a vice (pad the jaws to avoid damaging the shaft) while releasing it. Strong circlip pliers are a must for this, as it is an incredibly tight fit. Once sprung out, the circlip can then be removed and the joint itself tapped off. A concave washer fits beneath the joint, with the concave side towards the joint, which can also be removed.

Clean the splined end of the axle

shaft and replace the rubber gaiter if it looks at all suspect. Coloured high-grade copolymer gaiters or standard rubber gaiters are easily available and will prevent any future problems. The gaiter has to be fitted, obviously, before the concave washer and new joint is positioned on the axle. Ensure you fit the new CV joint with the unstepped side of the joint outer cage towards the gaiter. The stepped side has to face towards the stub-axle flange or gearbox drive flange or it won't fit. When fitting the new CV, tap it on using a tubular drift or socket bearing on the inner race. It is all too easy to hammer the outer cage which may not only cause damage, but may well also open the joint up to its maximum travel and shower the new, precision-made steel bearings all over your garage floor. If any dirt does get into the bearing, it will have to be cleaned off, packed with 60 grams of fresh molybdenum CV grease and the process started again.

Locate the securing circlip back in the groove (a new one is best as they have a tendency to distort when removed) and repeat the whole operation at the other end of the shaft. To prevent the ingress of water between the gaiter and axle shaft, either affix the metal clip that comes with most replacement gaiters, or seal the end with a rubber solution, such as Dow Corning. The compound used for sealing aquaria is particularly good. The rest of the operation is a reversal of the disassembly process.

Uprated units

One way to ensure longevity of the CV joints is to upgrade them to stronger units. The larger diameter (100mm) VW Type 2 Bus or Type 4 (411 or 412) models use a more durable CV. The Type 2 joint is the same diameter as the Type 4 unit, but is deeper, at 35mm, thus allowing extra movement. It can operate at angles up to 19 degrees intermittently, and 17 degrees on a continuous basis. These CV joints can be sourced secondhand or bought brand new, and are a worthwhile investment. The question then is how to fit them to the Beetle.

VW have already provided the answer, as the gearbox drive flanges fitted to the later VW 181 (Thing/Trekker) model will accommodate the CV joints at the inner end. These IRS flanges are easily removed, by prising out a centre cap and removing a

VW 181 (Thing/Trekker) gearbox drive flanges allow the use of stronger and larger Type 2 CV joints at the inner end of the IRS axle-shaft.

Porsche 944 diagonal A-arms will fit in place of the Beetle units, and allow the complete rear disc assembly and drive shafts from the Porsche to be used. Inner pivot bushes will have to be changed, and urethane replacements are ideal.

retaining circlip, before replacing them with the 181 flanges which are still available from VW dealers.

At the outer end, the Beetle stub-axle will have to be replaced with one sourced from a Porsche 924 or 944. These use the same length and spline arrangement as the Beetle, but have a larger drive flange which will accommodate the larger CV joints. These stub-axles, and indeed the whole diagonal A-arms to which they fit, can be substituted for the Beetle items, and they are readily available on the secondhand market. If you intend to fit the complete arms, then the inner pivot bush will need to be changed for VW items or, ideally, stronger heavy-duty urethane aftermarket items which will help rid the Beetle of sloppiness in the rear suspension which causes poor handling.

One problem that becomes apparent when attempting to fit the Type 2 CV joints to the Beetle axle shaft is that their width prevents them sliding right on to the splines of the shaft before they abut the axle shaft shoulder. Whilst it is possible to machine the shoulder down, this considerably weakens the shaft. The

alternative is to machine the inner face of the CV joint so that it sits further on to the Beetle axle shaft. It is just the centre part of the joint that requires modification, so that the CV joint will slip far enough on to the axle shaft splines to enable the fitting of the spring clip on the outside of the CV joint. This will then provide the correct overall length of axle shaft and joints to fit between the 181 output flanges and the Porsche stub-axles.

A somewhat more expensive alternative is to buy heavy-duty aftermarket axle shafts, such as those supplied by Sway-A-Way, Dura Blue, or Summers Brothers in the US. These axles have extra-long splines to suit the width of alternative CV joints, and allow the axle shaft to float within the inner CV joint races, thus facilitating a greater range of movement. They also allow a certain amount of twist, somewhat akin to that in the torsion-bars, which cushions loads and prevents damage to the CV joints and transaxle.

FITTING PORSCHE STUB-AXLES TO BEETLE A-ARMS

If you intend to fit just the Porsche stub-axles to the Beetle A-arms, this is the procedure to follow: The rear of the car must be jacked-up after the rear 36mm hub nuts and the wheel nuts have been loosened. Once on axle stands, the wheels can be taken off and the hub nuts removed. On each side, the brake drum can be drawn off, and the bearing cover and four retaining bolts holding each cover are then visible. Remove the bolts, and prise off the cover and the rubber 'O-ring' beneath it. The whole drum backplate, complete with internal components, can then be pulled away from the axle shaft. The handbrake cable and brake line can be left attached and the backplate supported to prevent overstretching the line, unless the brakes are also to be upgraded, in which case they should be removed completely.

The axle shaft can then be removed from the A-arm by using a bearing puller with the legs secured over the bearing housing flange on the A-arm whilst the screw thread is wound down and the shaft forced out. A less desirable option is to knock the stub-axle out with a soft-faced hammer and a block of wood as a cushion to prevent damage to the axle shaft thread. The inner spacer can then be slid off the shaft.

At the rear of each housing, the inner grease seal has to be prised out, taking care not to damage the mating surface where it sits in the housing. Beneath it is a strong circlip that holds the ball bearing in place, and this has to removed using circlip pliers. Once the circlip is sprung out, the bearing can be knocked out from the other side of the hub by tapping around the edge of the bearing race with a suitable drift to keep it square whilst sliding out.

The metal spacer sleeve that sits within the housing can then be removed, followed by the inner race of the roller bearing. The outer race can then be drifted out completely.

Reassembly, but with the Porsche stub-axles, is very much a reversal of the above process. Firstly, drive in the ball bearing race until it reaches its stop within the diagonal arm housing. The chamfered edge of the bearing outer race should face outwards. Then snap in the circlip, which must lie perfectly flat in its groove. You may need to replace the circlip if it does not line up properly and seat exactly, due to twisting upon removal. A new grease seal can then be tapped in, with the lip facing inwards.

Pack the bearing cavity with 60 – 80 grams (3 ounces) of high melting-point multipurpose grease, making sure that it is worked into the ball bearing and around the lip of the seal. Slip the inner spacer over your Porsche stub-axle, ensuring that the chamfered edge is the right way around to meet up with the radius of the shaft flange. The stub-axle can then be fitted into the housing from the back, tapping it into place through the ball bearing until the flange just meets the inner race. The metal spacer sleeve then slides over the axle shaft, followed by the roller bearing which must have the chamfered edge facing out. The inner race of this bearing is then fitted over the shaft and a drift, such as a suitably sized metal tube, must be used to tap it home. The bearing cover can then be re-attached with its four bolts once the brake backplate is positioned, having first replaced the rubber 'O-ring' around the housing lip, the bearing cover seal

if it is worn in any way, and the outer spacer. The double lip of the bearing cover should be filled with grease to lubricate the axle shaft.

The axle shaft and CV joints can then be mounted, ideally using new hex-headed bolts to prevent problems with stripping the delicate internal head next time they are removed. These pass through the metal spreader plates to even out the pressure of the bolts as they are torqued down.

Fitting Porsche 944 rear disc brakes

Having fitted the Porsche stub-axles, it also makes sense to consider exchanging the Beetle rear drum brakes for the ventilated rear disc brake setup from the Porsche 944 at the same time. As with many operations described in this book, there are several options. You may wish to fit the disc setup to the rebuilt Beetle A-arms we have just described above, or you may wish to simply

Later versions of the Porsche 944 had cast alloy rear A-arms and Porsche 928-type twin-pot calipers, but these are relatively scarce.

transplant the A-arms and complete rear braking components from the Porsche onto the Beetle chassis. The Porsche 944 has a very similar rear suspension design to the semi-automatic, 1302 and 1303 IRS Beetles, and was introduced to the UK market as far back as 1982, making secondhand parts a cost-effective proposition. Later versions of the 944 even had cast alloy rear A-arms and Porsche 928-type twin-pot calipers, but you would be extremely lucky to find these at a realistic price.

Those we will look at here, however, were fitted with radially ventilated discs of 289mm diameter and 20mm thickness. The discs also come fitted with a cable operated handbrake mechanism, using a 180mm diameter internal twin-shoe drum brake arrangement, working on the inner face of the disc hub. This ensures the mechanism is legal when converted on to the Beetle.

The A-arms are almost identical in design to the Beetle items apart from a slight difference in the bolting pattern to the spring-plate, and the inner pivot bush, which will have to be changed for a Beetle item. A urethane bush, suitably greased, is the ideal replacement, and should be pressed in using a vice or hydraulic press. Even the torsion-bars are interchangeable.

Fitting the complete A-arm assemblies from the Porsche should be undertaken when the vehicle is also having other work done to it, such as lowering. The process for this is identical in principle to that of the swing-axle Beetles, and requires the disassembly of the spring-plates from the A-arms, thus providing an ideal opportunity to change the A-arms and braking components at the same time. The A-arms themselves are removed from the chassis once the inner pivot pin is removed. This requires the use

Removing the A-arm inner pivot pin requires the use of a special 19mm Allen-headed key, which can also be used to remove the gearbox drain and fill plugs.

of a special Allen-headed key, the same size as is used to undo the gearbox drain plug.

For those wishing to severely lower the rear suspension of their IRS Beetles, you will find that static negative camber will be caused at the rear wheels unless the A-arms are swapped over, left to right. This is possible once the shock absorber mountings are cut off each and re-welded in to the same position relative to the chassis on the transplanted arm.

Despite their similar visual appearance, the two arms have different alignments within the chassis, and 'handing' them in this way will allow the rear suspension to sit in a position of more neutral camber than before, thus giving better handling.

Removing the Porsche rear suspension and brakes

If you are sourcing Porsche parts from a breaker's yard, and taking them off the vehicle yourself, this is the procedure you will need to follow. As with a Beetle, slacken the rear hub nut before raising the rear of the vehicle. The cotter pin comes out before the nut is loosened, except on the alloy trailing-arm models, where a cotter pin is not used. The 944 is often fitted with thick wheel spacers behind the

The Porsche 944 rear disc slides on to the stub-axle splines like a Beetle drum. The inner friction surface allows the handbrake shoes to operate on the inside part of the disc. (Courtesy Total VW magazine).

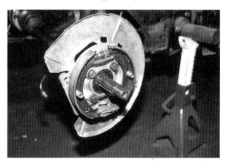

The Porsche 944 handbrake mechanism is compact, but efficient. Replacement brake shoes from a BMW are considerably cheaper than the Porsche equivalents. (Courtesy Total VW magazine).

wheels, and these will need to be slid off the wheel studs once the wheels are removed.

The disc is held to the hub by a number of small countersunk retaining screws, which must be removed. The caliper itself is mounted by two rear-mounted bolts to a cast aluminium mounting. Once unbolted, the caliper can be swung out of the way. The disc should then pull from the studs freely. If it sticks, the shoes of the handbrake are not completely released. Backing the shoes off is a matter of inserting a screwdriver through the access hole in the disc centre to turn the star adjuster within. If it still sticks, a couple of bolts should be inserted into the threaded guides provided, and turned down until the disc is forced off the hub. The rear hub should then slide off the splines without the use of a puller, as it should have been greased with a moly-based grease when fitting.

Behind the hub sits the hand-brake mechanism, which is not unlike a Beetle setup, and consists of a pair of shoes fitted with hold-down springs to locate them on to the backing plate. A single, central top-mounted brake shoe adjuster, horizontally-mounted return springs, and a bottom-mounted operating lever for the handbrake cable complete the setup.

The handbrake cable mounts to the brake shoe actuating (operating) lever and must first be released from the lever and pulled through the backing plate. The handbrake cable must be released where it mounts to the handbrake lever next to the driver's seat, by undoing the locking and adjusting nuts from the cable end. The cable branches into two where it goes through the body, and it must be detached from its mounting clips to finally free the cable from the body. Since you will require two nearside (longer length) cables, ensure you get these at the same time, as part of the deal you negotiate at the breaker's yard.

The hold-down springs retaining the brake shoes are then pressed down and turned to release them. Do not lose the springs or the star adjuster at the top. The shoes themselves should be replaced with new items upon reassembly, and it is worth noting that those from a BMW will fit, but are much cheaper than Porsche items. With all the brake components out of the way, you will see a central bearing housing held by four bolts, which is identical to the IRS Beetle.

A Porsche rear disc brake setup on a Beetle chassis. Ventilated discs and large four-po[...] calipers give, perhaps, the ultimate high performance rear braking capacity to a Beetle.

This must be removed, and this also frees the backing plate which provides the location for the brake shoes and the caliper mount. The light alloy brake splash plates are not usually in a very good condition, but sit behind this backing plate/caliper mount. They either need to be replaced upon reassembly, or left off to improve cooling, though they are there to prevent damage to the discs and do have a valid function. A rubber 'O-ring' is the last component that fits on to the diagonal A-arm, and should also be replaced upon reassembly.

As you will see, the diagonal A-arm that is attached to the Porsche donor is removed in much the same way as it would be on a Beetle, once the CV joints and drive-shafts are removed between the stub-axles and gearbox drive flanges. If you are not using Type 2 CV joints, you will also need the Porsche CV joints on the outer ends, at least, to match the

larger drive flanges.

As the brake lines will be renewed, it is not necessary to worry too much about the method of removing them, though you may wish to keep the rigid line running to the Porsche caliper to use as a pattern when making a new one. Also retain the horseshoe-shaped brake line retainers that locate the unions between the flexible and rigid brake pipes, as these are needed.

With a chisel, mark a line across the top of the A-arm mounting plate (as you would when de-cambering a Beetle), prior to releasing the retaining bolts through the mounting plate and spring-plate. On the Porsche 944, a rear stabilizer bar also attaches to a pair of special bolts at this point, and must also be released. Although this bar can be used on your Beetle, together with the original brackets and new mounts that will have to be especially fabricated, it is better to use an aftermarket heavy-duty anti-roll bar. We shall look at this later on.

Finally, the A-arm inner pivot nut and bolt can be undone using a socket and spanner, and the A-arm removed from the vehicle.

The two rubber bushings held by the eye of the arm are the ones that have to be replaced with Beetle or urethane aftermarket items. They can be pressed out or driven out with a hammer and cold chisel applied from side to side to drift them squarely out of the bushing cavity. With all the Porsche parts removed, any overhaul work that is needed will now have to be done prior to installing the parts onto your Beetle. The discs themselves should be checked carefully to ensure they are free from damage, and within the limits of wear tolerance.

The caliper disc pads should obviously be changed as a matter of course, and the whole caliper thoroughly cleaned. A spring lock has to be removed from the rear side of the caliper to allow the pad retaining pins to be withdrawn. A fine drift is the best tool to knock the pins out without damaging the pins or the caliper. The inner pad should be removed first, once the piston has been pressed back into the cylinder as far as possible to release it. The outer pad will still remain pressed between the caliper frame and the disc, and a pry-bar should be used to ease the two apart before pulling it back out of the caliper body. If you use a screwdriver, ensure it does not damage the disc. The pad can then be removed. If a full rebuild of the caliper is to be undertaken, then a workshop manual should be consulted, and the correct rebuild kit obtained. Alternatively, exchange rebuilt calipers are available at a reasonable price.

The fitting process on to the Beetle is a reverse procedure to that of

dismantling on the Porsche, allowing for the change to the inner pivot bushes, and any other modifications that you wish to make at this point, such as fitting the Type 2 CV joints and VW 181 gearbox drive flanges and modified axle shafts. The one thing that will have to be considered in all cases is the fitting of the handbrake cables.

The handbrake

Firstly, take the outer handbrake cables from the Beetle, and cut off the curved end that goes into the Beetle brake backplate. Then hold the similar type of Porsche end in a vice, and work the cable until it pulls out of the metal fitting. Taking the outer Beetle cable, de-burr the cut end, and carefully work it into the Porsche fitting. This should locate and remain secure by itself, but an epoxy compound helps seal the joint.

Moving to the inner cables, use the two longer Porsche nearside cables that were sourced. These will have to be cut so that they are exactly the same length as the Beetle items, once an end is fitted on. Always work out the length of the cable before cutting it. The easiest way to do this is to fit all the other components up on the chassis and push the cables up through the chassis so they protrude at the handbrake. Pull them through with a pair of Mole grips or pliers to take up any slack, and mark the cable. Allow for the length of the connector itself, and the fact that the cable end will push up into the connector. You can either use cable connectors from a dune buggy cable shortening kit, or buy a pair of crimp-on ends, which are stronger. In the case of the latter, these have to be M6 bolt size, of 50mm length with an central inner hole of 2.75mm into which the cut Porsche cable end is inserted. These connec-

tors are available from specialist cable suppliers such as Speedy Cables in the UK.

The cable end should be heated up with a blowtorch until it is glowing red, and can then be inserted into the new connector which can be held in a vice. The combination of the heated cable, and pressure applied with the vice being tightened up, will crimp the end on.

Porsche brakes

With the handbrake mechanism sorted out and adapted to its new home, the Porsche brake parts can be rebuilt on to the diagonal A-arm once it is fitted into place within the Beetle chassis. The new (BMW) brake shoes have to be located with their hold-down springs. These are depressed with a pair of pliers and the straight portion inserted through the slot in the backing plate and twisted to securely fasten them. The return springs are also added, and the handbrake operating lever and strut assembly fitted within the locators in the bottom of the shoes. This mechanism should be greased to prevent friction, making sure that it does not find its way on to the brake shoe linings.

The adjuster is fitted at the top of the brake shoes, with the star wheel positioned towards the front. The brake shoes will have to be eased apart slightly to allow the adjuster to seat correctly between them. The disc can then be fitted, turning the star adjuster as necessary to help clear the shoes inside. The locating screws can then be fitted to hold the disc in place, and the caliper attached to the mount at the rear of the disc. Since the brake lines will all have to be replaced, it means that the whole brake system will have to be purged of air, once the whole operation is completed. Stainless steel braided flexible pipes, and

Using Porsche discs means a change of wheels, to the smaller PCD (pitch circle diameter) Porsche five-stud pattern. With this level of engineering, who wants to hide it behind stock Beetle wheels anyway?

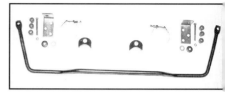

The Sway-A-Way heavy-duty rear anti-roll bar comes complete with urethane bushings and stainless-steel clamps. The bar helps prevent body-roll, and can be used to complement a similar front bar.

copper rigid pipes are the best options as they combine high performance with good looks.

Once the wheels are fitted (and you will now have to use Porsche wheels or ones with a Porsche PCD wheel stud pattern to match the Porsche wheel studs), the 36mm retaining hub nut will have to be torqued up to 217lb/ft. **Caution!** Always ensure the car is off the axle stands before attempting this, and use a long extension bar to give the socket maximum leverage. Alternatively, use the Torque-Meister tool described at the beginning of the book. If the width of the 7 inch wide Porsche wheel is too much for the wheelarches of your Beetle, you may wish to use the narrower 5 1/2in wheel. In this case the large spacer that is normally fitted behind the wheel should be omitted, and the long wheel studs will require replacement with those from a Porsche fitted with 45mm studs.

Dependant on the other changes made to the braking system of your Beetle, you may wish to fit a brake proportioning valve into the braking circuit if you use the Porsche 944 rear disc setup. This is simply because the brake bias of the Beetle and the Porsche 944 is set up on the original vehicles slightly differently due to the location of the engine (the 944 being front-engined).

ANTI-ROLL (ANTI-SWAY) BARS

Whether you wish to fit a Porsche independent rear suspension to your Beetle, or only the brakes, or leave it standard, there is another modification that can really help the handling of the IRS rear suspension. Fitting an anti-roll, or anti-sway bar, prevents the body roll that is common on an unmodified Beetle, and this must be used in conjunction with an uprated

front anti-roll bar. Such bars are available from US companies such as Sway-A-Way and other suppliers, and also have the benefit of being fitted with urethane bushes for longevity and strength.

The Sway-A-Way bar is a hefty 5/8in diameter, shaped to fit under the transaxle. It is mounted using stainless steel clamps to the torsion-bar housing on either side of the floorpan, and to link brackets affixed to the spring-plate mountings. Curved urethane mountings locate between the anti-roll bar and the clamps on the torsion housings for solid support. Link bolts, nuts, urethane bushings and cupped washers attach the bar to the link brackets.

It is easiest to fit this setup whilst the Beetle is having the Porsche 944 diagonal A-arms attached to the Beetle spring-plates, or during lowering, when the suspension is just being rebuilt. As you will need good access to the underside of the car, make sure the car is up on axle stands, and on a flat surface. Clean the bottom side of the torsion-bar housings along the bottom edge, as this is where the cupped urethane washers make contact.

In order to install the anti-roll bar, first locate the three rear spring-plate bolts, and remove the ones that will go through the anti-roll bar link plate. Some Beetles only have upper and lower bolts in this position, and the

An anti-roll bar fitted to Beetle IRS rear suspension. A shaped plate bolts through the spring-plate and A-arm mountings, and runs transversely under the torsion-bar tubes.

link plate itself will dictate where a third bolt will have to be drilled through the A-arm mounting. If the A-arm is being reset in relation to the spring-plate at this point, always ensure that the toe-in measurement is set to 1/32in before any drilling is carried out. Place the link bracket, which fixes the outer end of the anti-roll bar to the spring-plate, flat against the outside of the plate so that the bottom part of the bracket passes under the spring-plate (towards the centre of the car). Do this on each side of the car.

When reinstalling the spring-plate bolts, you will find that the width of the plate and washers, combined with the width of the A-arm mounting and spring-plate, prevents the nut from holding on to the bolt securely. You'll need to fit the longer bolts from a swing-axle Beetle rear suspension, and then torque them up to 80ft/lb. Grease the insides of the curved urethane bushings and slip them on to the sway bar. The bushings are split on one

edge to easily facilitate this. Fit them just inside the large bend, but on the straight portion of the bar. Seat the bearings against the bottom of the torsion housings, and loosely assemble the steel straps around them.

Centre the bar on the torsion housings and lift the ends of the bar until they meet the link brackets. The links assemble with the link bolt running through a curved washer and urethane bushing, the bracket itself, the eye of the anti-roll bar and another bushing and washer. The whole assembly is held by a nut torqued to 5lb/ft. Before tightening the steel straps around the torsion housings, lower the car onto the ground so that the anti-roll bar aligns itself correctly.

TYRE CLEARANCE

Before we leave the Beetle IRS rear suspension, there is a final modification that is of interest to those building a dune buggy. If large rear tyres are used, there is potentially a

problem of tyre clearance on the torsion-bar housings. On an IRS Beetle, these are the longer length 26 9/16in bars that provide the later Beetles with a softer handling. However, like the earliest Beetles that also used longer torsion-bars, they stick out from the spring-plate retaining cover by several inches.

The solution is to exchange the bars with those of a swing-axle Beetle, which are shorter at 21 3/4in. To enable them to locate to the diagonal A-arm of the IRS Beetle, the swing-axle spring-plate will also be required. Since this is longer, it will have to be shortened and shaped at the end that attaches to the diagonal A-arm. It will also have to have the elongated mounting slots to allow toe-in adjustment drilled through them. This is a job for a qualified machine shop, and should not be done if the measurements will be less than 100% accurate. As the plates are to be used on a buggy, you may also wish to use aftermarket plates designed for heavy-duty off-road use, and there are many to choose from, including the US-made Summers Brothers plates. Again, these will need to be bought as spring-plates for the swing-axle Beetle and modified to suit this particular application.

OBTAINING PARTS

The Beetle design allows for a huge diversity of parts interchangeability and modification as we have already seen. In all cases, the emphasis should be on thinking through the type of changes you will want to make before actually starting anything. Firstly, this is simply good planning, since it ensures you do not have to tackle a major job twice, and you can plan a series of jobs that have the same basic starting point. The second issue is simply the question of time and money. You can save a lot of time by locating parts from dealers (or even secondhand from specialist breakers) in one operation, rather than returning time and time again. You may also be able to secure a better price for yourself by doing things this way. However, if only one job is to be tackled at a time, then parts can be purchased in a logical step-by-step way to spread the cost.

Shop around for the best prices with dealers, and also check the small ads sections of enthusiasts' magazines. You may well be able to find the parts that you are looking for at greatly discounted prices.

Finally, with the thriving show scene for the air-cooled VW enthusiast, go to as many events as possible and check out the bargains on new and secondhand parts at the swapmeet section.

Chapter 4
The chassis

The Beetle chassis/floorpan is the foundation for the rest of the car, as it provides the mounting for the suspensions, gearbox and engine, and the bodyshell. Complete with suspensions, wheels and tyres, the floorpan forms an independent rolling chassis, consisting of a central backbone, 140mm wide and 165mm high, which provides much of the strength for the assembled car when the body is mounted to it. The front frame-head widens to accept the four mounting bolts for the front axle assembly, steering and brakes, and the U-shaped fork at the rear supports the transmission and drive shafts. The engine bolts to the bellhousing of the gearbox, but is otherwise unsupported. Welded on either side of the central backbone are the floor pans which carry the runners for the seats, the mounting for the battery, and the support for the pedal assembly.

The very simplicity of the chassis design makes it an ideal candidate for

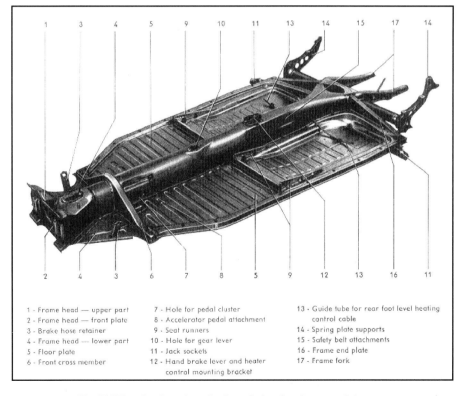

1 - Frame head — upper part
2 - Frame head — front plate
3 - Brake hose retainer
4 - Frame head — lower part
5 - Floor plate
6 - Front cross member
7 - Hole for pedal cluster
8 - Accelerator pedal attachment
9 - Seat runners
10 - Hole for gear lever
11 - Jack sockets
12 - Hand brake lever and heater control mounting bracket
13 - Guide tube for rear foot level heating control cable
14 - Spring plate supports
15 - Safety belt attachments
16 - Frame end plate
17 - Frame fork

The VW Beetle chassis – the foundation for the rest of the car. (Courtesy Walter Bach).

The VW Beetle chassis has made the ideal foundation for kit-cars and specials through the years. Shortened chassis are needed for some kits, such as the Porsche Speedster and Spyder models, as well as dune buggies. (Courtesy Chesil Motor Company).

re-bodying with bodyshells of different designs, such as kit-cars or dune buggies. It also means that a restorer can physically remove the Beetle bodyshell from the chassis to allow unrivalled access to both parts before reassembly. Whether the body is to be restored or discarded to allow kit construction, the method of removal is much the same. We will look at this first before venturing into more radical chassis work such as floorpan shortening, floorpan replacement, frame-head repair or exchange and converting a swing-axle Beetle to IRS.

REMOVING THE VW BEETLE BODYSHELL

The first job is to remove all items from the interior of the Beetle, such as the seats, floormats, seat belts and the battery, which is situated under the rear seat. If the body is not to be reused, the next step is to remove as much weight as possible to make the job of lifting the body from the chassis as easy as possible. This includes all the wings, bonnet, engine lid, bumpers and doors, which are all bolt-on items. Whilst most of these can be dismantled using spanners or a socket to release the bolts, the doors can sometimes be tricky as the cross-head bolts are invariably too tight to remove with a cross-head screwdriver. A cross-head socket attachment on an impact driver tool is the best way to loosen these bolts. The check strap on the door also requires the removal of a retaining pin to release it.

Moving to the front of the car, remove the cardboard liner in the under-bonnet area to access the fuel tank. Besides being a safety factor, it is necessary to remove the tank to access the body bolts attaching the front of the body to the front suspension. The filler vent hose and fuel gauge sender wire should be pulled off the tank, and the four bolts and metal tabs that locate the tank removed. The tank can then be lifted slightly to reach the petrol pipe underneath, which must be plugged immediately to prevent fuel spillage. As a precaution, place the tank well away from the area where you are working. **Caution!** It is the fumes given off by the petrol, rather than the liquid itself, that are explosive, so never take any chances. Once the tank is removed you will see the two hex-headed nuts that hold the front of the body to the front axle assembly, and these must be removed.

Whilst at the front, unbolt the steering column collar where it mounts to the steering box and remove the horn wire. Unclip the metal 'stop' at the top of the collapsible section of the steering column (on later Beetles), to allow the column to be pulled back off the steering box splines. Inside the car, a 'U–shaped' bracket with two bolts mounts to the underside of the dashboard (it is integral with the steering column on later cars), along with a wiring harness which must be labelled and un-hooked. The steering column can then be given a bit of friendly persuasion to pull it from the splines of the steering coupler spider.

You will also need to disconnect the speedometer cable from the front left wheel hub and pull it clear of the wheel assembly. Also disconnect the wires from the brake master-cylinder switches and pull off the flexible hoses from the brake fluid reservoir where they connect to the master cylinder inlet elbows. Be prepared to mop up any fluid that spills out as it is corrosive.

The next job is to free any electrical connections which may interfere with the removal of the body. These are mainly concentrated in the engine bay, such as the wiring to the ignition coil, generator and oil pressure switch. Underneath the car, the fuel line needs to be disconnected and plugged, if there is any fuel still in the pipe. The rubber hose tends to harden with age and may need to be cut free. The concertina heater hose pipes also have to be removed. These somewhat bulky items run between the heat exchangers at each side of the engine, and the rear of the car body where they attach to a fitting made of a bakelite material. They may need some persuading to come free, but do not damage the fittings (if attempting a restoration) as they are difficult to replace.

If the Beetle body is to be scrapped, the body can literally be cut into pieces once the window glass has been removed. Cuts should be made through the roof pillars and the base of the door apertures. The car can be also turned on its side to facilitate access to the bolts that run around the perimeter of the floorpan and hold the body in place. If you do choose this method, remember to drain the gearbox oil and remove the engine before attempting to tip the vehicle up. You will also need to support the chassis before the last bolts are removed or it will fall back on you. Never attempt this type of disassembly single-handed, as the weight of the chassis, and body, is far greater than one person can manage.

For a vehicle being restored, such drastic measures should not be taken, and the car must be kept on all four wheels whilst the body is released. Only 32 bolts secure the body, and the majority run in a channel on the underside perimeter of the floorpan. As you remove them save the rectangular washers that spread the load of the bolts, as these will be reused.

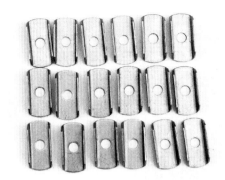

The rectangular washers which spread the load of the Beetle bodyshell mounting bolts can be changed for stainless-steel items for good looks and durability.

Alternatively, you may exchange these for stainless-steel aftermarket items upon reassembly, which will both look nicer and last indefinitely.

Bolts will also be found across the rear section of the floorpan inside the car, underneath where the rear seat was located, and these are easy to undo, having never been subjected to the ravages of weather. Those most often overlooked are the 17mm ones located in the rear wheel arches (behind the wheels and tyres) which mount directly to the top of the rear suspension casting. These are often the worst two bolts to undo in the whole of the car, as the bolt heads will have rusted, and tend to round off easily when a spanner is applied. If a releasing fluid does not help, or the bolts shear off, this causes more work to remove them.

If the bolts shear flush with the suspension casting, you will have no choice but to drill the stud out and re-tap the thread when the body is removed. However, the bolt usually shears with around 1/8in of thread standing proud of the casting. Dab a little weld onto this (or get a welder to perform this part of the work for you). The heat will 'unlock' the frozen bolt, and the added weld will provide

something to grip on to. Use Mole grips (or similar) to then wind the bolt shank out. You can even perform this operation from underneath to remove a flush-sheared bolt, and then wind it out right through the suspension casting.

From here on, it's a case of lifting the body up and off the floorpan. VW used a lifting device to raise a body from the chassis, but you will have to either use a hoist to lift the body up, or physically lift it off. In the former operation, you will need a garage with roof members strong enough to support the body weight on a hoist, and with enough height to clear the chassis completely, so it can be rolled out from underneath it. The body can then be lowered onto padded blocks – assuming it is going to be restored – to prevent accidental damage on the ground. The latter method requires the use of some strong friends to physically lift the body clear of the chassis. Even in a stripped-down form, never underestimate the weight of the body, especially on earlier cars.

1302/03 Beetles
The instructions I have given so far relate to the removal of the Beetle bodyshell from a torsion-bar type floorpan. However, there are some differences concerning the disassembly of the front suspension mounting from the MacPherson strut-equipped 1302/03 Beetles. The bodyshell is attached by the usual body/chassis bolts but, in addition, there are two more on top of the central tunnel near the front bulkhead which must be removed. Under the bonnet there are three nuts on the top of both MacPherson assemblies which have to be released, as must the two chassis bolts that hide beneath two plastic caps where the spare tyre is housed. Underneath the car are three bolts that hold the

A Beetle rolling chassis stripped of its original bodyshell. Whether you are restoring the Beetle, or using the chassis beneath a kit, access to everything is now much easier. Use the opportunity!

steering idler arm behind the struts themselves, and these must also be removed. Looking towards the front of the 'hammerhead' section of the chassis you will see two corner bolts that must be undone. Finally, unbolt the steering arm under the wing of the driver's side, behind the MacPherson strut. The body is now free to be released. We will look at the modification of this type of floorpan later on.

Access to everything on the chassis is 100% easier with the body removed, so use the opportunity to make any changes to the chassis whilst it is in this denuded state. We are going to begin with one of the most drastic pieces of surgery possible on a VW floorpan: shortening it.

SHORTENING THE FLOORPAN

Whether you build a dune buggy, or any other type of kit-car – such as the very popular Porsche Spyder replica - that requires a shortened VW floorpan, you will have to consider the prospect of shortening the chassis. Such modifications are not a new concept.

The dune buggy craze in the mid 1960s fuelled a demand for this type of modification that not only made the finished vehicle look more purposeful in its abbreviated form, but also increased the manoeuvrability and ground clearance. It also gave an incredibly tight turning circle and better responsiveness to the car.

Volkswagenwerk took note of these modifications, and issued a factory instruction manual in September 1969 for those wishing to shorten the Type 1 (Beetle) frame for a Karmann GF or IMP dune buggy, thereby endorsing such modifications to the basic platform chassis design.

A Beetle chassis prepared to accept a dune buggy bodyshell. The simplicity and strength of the rolling chassis design has made it ideal for building buggies. (Courtesy John Jackson).

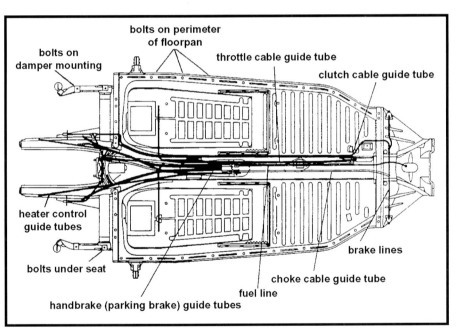

A diagram of the cable conduits within the central backbone of the Beetle chassis. (Courtesy Cars & Car Conversions magazine).

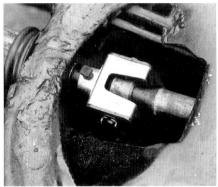

The rear access plate is removed to allow the gearbox 'hockey stick' selector to be disengaged from the long gear selector rod which runs within the chassis backbone.

With the gearbox and gear-shifter removed, the selector rod can be physically pushed from its resting place in the plastic support bush with a long rod inserted through the rear section of the chassis.

With the Beetle bodyshell removed from the floorpan, the basic running gear is still attached. To make the floorpan more manoeuvrable in the workshop, and to gain access to the various parts, it is necessary to remove the large assemblies such as the engine, gearbox and front suspension from the floorpan. Also remove the pedal cluster, gear lever, gear coupling and gear selector rod within the backbone tunnel, front and rear tunnel access plates, and the clutch cable flexible guide tube.

The reason for the removal of the access plates is that the gear selector rod has to be physically pushed from its resting place within a plastic support bushing inside a metal bracket mounted to the top of the tunnel. This is situated just behind the gear lever mounting, accessible when the gearstick itself, together with the spring and metal guide plate, is removed by releasing the two bolts. The selector rod, once freed from the coupling with the gearbox 'hockey stick' at the rear, can be pushed forward with a long metal or wooden rod through the round hole seen at the rear of the chassis, between the frame forks. The selector rod will travel forward and catch on the inside of the front frame-head. Putting your hand through the opening normally covered by the front access plate, and turning the rod through 180 degrees, will allow the mount at the front of the rod for the gear lever to pass through the access hole. The rod can then be fully with-drawn.

The gear selector rod will need to be shortened by the same amount as the rest of the chassis. A hacksaw can be used to cut it, but it must be accurately aligned together for re-welding. A slight bevelling of the two mating edges will allow better weld penetration, and the joint will need to be smoothed off before refitting. When it is eventually pushed back into the locating bush, it must be greased freely with a universal grease. It is also worthwhile changing the plastic bush for a new one, as these wear and are often damaged on older cars. The bush is located in a suspended bracket within the tunnel and (on most mod-els) uses an expanding metal ring at its leading edge to eliminate shift rod noise. It is tricky to fit, but a worth-while operation whilst the opportunity is available to you.

Before going further, now is the time to consider the suspension arrangements you wish to have on the finished vehicle. It may be perfectly acceptable to you to have a car with the front king and link-pin or ball-joint type front suspension, and a swing axle rear. In that case you will just be thinking of the shortening process. However, if you wish to mix and match suspensions, now is the ideal time to do so, as the chassis will be cut apart.

There are several options open to you. Unless you have been lucky enough to find an American-spec.

chassis with a ball-joint front suspen-sion and IRS rear (which will be left-hand drive), or a semi-automatic transmission type chassis (which will not have a conventional clutch cable guide tube, and will therefore require the use of an hydraulic clutch assem-bly), you will have to build a hybrid chassis.

You may wish to add mounts for the IRS diagonal A-arms to an other-wise swing-axle floorpan, and this can be done after the shortening process. This will also allow you to use the rear suspension from the Porsche 944, as we have already seen. Alternatively, you can shorten an IRS floorpan, and then exchange the front frame-head for that of the earlier type of torsion-bar chassis. Finally, you can use the front section of a torsion-bar chassis mated to the rear section of an IRS floorpan. We will return to look at the first two options later in the chapter, but it is the latter method that con-cerns us here, whilst we are physically cutting a floorpan in two, ready for shortening.

With chassis shortening, the golden rules are accuracy of measure-ment, and the need to work on a flat floor. Begin by cleaning the floorpan as much as possible, and use chisels to remove the sound deadening material from the floorpan around the area that you will be working on. This is effec-tively everything rearward of the handbrake mounting. It is a tar-board type of material, and is time-consum-ing to scrape off, but all traces of it must be removed as it will otherwise catch fire when you are welding the floorpan. Since there can be some variation in body sizes, even between the same type of glassfibre kit, always trial-fit your buggy or kit-car body to the floorpan and see if the instructions give the correct length for cutting.

For the purposes of this text we

The cable conduits are tack welded to the rear of the chassis, and on the frame forks. Tacks must be carefully broken so the conduits can be pushed through when the two parts of the shortened chassis are drawn together.

will assume the amount to be cut out is 16in, although it doesn't matter what length is removed so long as the basic principle is understood. The 16in will be measured behind the hand-brake on the central tunnel and marked. If you are adding an IRS rear floorpan section to the chassis, double check the positioning of the handbrake mounting on **both** floorpans, as they vary with the age of the Beetle.

Unless you are going to reuse the VW seat runners they can be removed by carefully breaking the spot welds with a cold chisel. The old Beetle jacking points, heater cable conduits and battery support post can also be removed. Any holes produced during their removal can be welded up later.

Turning your attention to the rear of the chassis, find where the outer housings for the control cables are welded to the chassis as they exit the rear and side of the central tunnel. Very carefully break the welds that hold them to the chassis, as they will be pushed through when the chassis is shortened. In the case of adding an IRS rear section, the conduits should still be freed in this manner and pushed into the new floorpan section when it is added. This avoids the need to join and sleeve two conduit sections

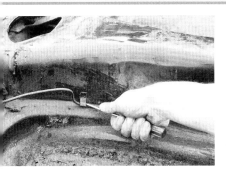

Brake lines must be moved from the area of the chassis that is to be shortened, and ideally should be replaced with new lines. The sound-deadening material needs to be scraped from the chassis.

In the centre of the floorpan which can give less than perfect runs for the cables, although those for the handbrake cables may have to be centrally joined due to their awkward location in the rear forks of the chassis.

Also at the rear, remove the main brake line from the brass 'T' fitting. Bend open the tabs along the side of the central tunnel from the rear to the vicinity of the handbrake, remove the rubber grommet on the floorpan and pull the brake line through, bending it forward without kinking it. If this, or any brake line, looks dubious, it should be replaced. With the chassis in this stripped state it is possible to inspect and replace parts easily, so don't miss the opportunity.

To make it easier to reach the handbrake cable conduits, the inspection hole at the rear of the chassis (underneath an oval-shaped plate with two location tongues, that also provides access to the gear shift coupling) can be enlarged by 1/2in.

You should also remove the floorpan to body sealing gasket around the perimeter of the floorpan. On early cars it is held by nails and breaks very easily. Later cars used a mastic to seal between the two surfaces, and this is bad news as it has to be scraped off, and is very difficult to

remove. A new floorpan gasket is essential when the time comes to lower the body on to the floorpan.

Before you begin the shortening process, check the floorpans for damage or rust. The most common area for problems is where the battery sits on the metal floorpan, any spilled acid eats through the metal. Equally, the side channels of the floorpans may have been damaged during the removal of the old body if a poor welding repair to the heater channels of the Beetle body physically joined the body to the floor. Sadly, this is a common problem, and only grinding or a cold chisel can then part the two. It is always better to retain the original pans if they are serviceable, as the original metal – particularly on pre-1966 Beetles - is much thicker and of a better quality than most 'pattern' floorpans available.

Floorpan sections can be replaced prior to actually shortening the chassis. Smaller sections are also available to repair localised damage or rusted areas. (Courtesy Chesil Motor Company).

Nevertheless, floorpans, or even just sections of floorpans, can be purchased quite readily and fitted quite easily. They can also be fitted to a complete Beetle where disassembly is not being undertaken, though the work required to position them is greater with the body still in place. If only the battery section has rotted, judicious shortening of the chassis may remove most of the bad metal anyway, so bear this in mind. If a full-length floorpan is to be fitted, this must be done prior to shortening the whole chassis to prevent any misalignment problems. If original VAG panels are obtainable, they are a safer bet, in terms of quality and fit, but obviously will be more expensive. Ensure that you have the correct panels for your year of chassis, and that they are set up for the driving position in your car – the driver's side will need the additional support for the accelerator pedal.

Begin removing the old panel by chiselling along the old floor panel next to the tunnel. The floor must also be released from the front and rear cross-members before it can be removed. The remaining strips of floor, still attached by spot welds to the tunnel flange, can then be carefully chiselled off and the flange dressed and cleaned up ready to accept the new floorpan. Once offered up into position, the floorpan will have to be plug-welded into position on the central tunnel flange, replacing the original spot-welds. This is simply because the gauge of the floorpan metal will be different to that of the tunnel, and conventional welding will simply melt the floorpan metal into a large hole before the tunnel metal melts enough to make a satisfactory weld between the two surfaces. An arc-welder can be used to do the job, by first drilling through both surfaces at regular intervals (to copy the original spot welds) and back-filling the joint with the welding rod. Conventional seam-welding can be used where the floor abuts the chassis cross-members front and rear. This is just one of the jobs on the welding of a chassis where specialist help, or tools, is recommended for anyone who is not a competent welder.

The fitting of part-panels, such as the rear section, or a half-length panel follows the same principle. Always measure carefully before cutting an old floorpan away, to ensure that the new one will abut all the mounting edges correctly for welding. Clean the edges so that the weld will penetrate properly, and seal all joints afterwards with seam sealer to prevent the ingress of water which would weaken the joint.

Cutting the chassis

The cutting now starts in earnest, so there's no turning back. Take plenty of care when measuring up the chassis prior to cutting it in half, and even more when welding it back together. There are several ways to mark-up a chassis ready for cutting. One method is to mark and cut a section straight across the floorpan behind the handbrake mounting, and where the seat runners were positioned, then cut a dart into the rear floorpan section to bring the semi-box section of the outside edge level. However, when completed, this allows the chassis to flex across one single, straight joint, and it is not recommended, though it is widely practiced, due to its simplicity.

The second method is to measure across the chassis in the same position as the first method, but to stagger the joint in one or more 'steps' across the floorpans to rid the shortened floorpan of the rear chassis taper that exists. This prevents a mismatch along the

perimeter of the pan, and provides additional welds to minimise flex across the joints. Nevertheless, the third method is the one we will look at here, and is accepted as being one of the strongest and safest methods of floorpan shortening: the 'herring-bone', or chevron pattern.

Looked at from above, the area that is to be removed from the floorpan resembles a herring-bone shape that runs across the central tunnel just behind the handbrake lever, and tapers rearwards across the back section of the floorpans into the corners of each pan. The reason for cutting at this angle is twofold: the longer welded area is much stronger than a straight cut since it prevents flexing of the joint; and the taper at the rear of the chassis is also accommodated. There is thus no mismatch of the two sections of floorpan when they are rejoined.

Begin by bending a piece of thin sheet metal, at least 4in wide by 14in long, around the tunnel to scribe against and ensure accuracy. A line should be marked 1-1½in behind the handbrake. Measure 16in back (or the amount your chassis has to be shortened by) and scribe a second line. Mark your chassis with masking tape in a herring bone/chevron shape back across the floorpans from the second line to the corner of the floorpan. Measure 16in forward on the perimeter of the floorpan, and mark a second chevron line parallel to the first across the floorpan, back to the first line marked on the tunnel. Initial rough cuts on the inside of the lines over the tunnel can be made with a cutting disc, whilst final, trimmed, edges can be achieved more accurately with a hacksaw.

Be especially careful not to cut any of the control cable conduits inside the centre of the tunnel, as

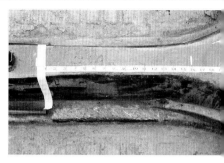

Mark a point about 1½in/38.1mm back from the handbrake mount, and a second point measured back from this by the amount that the chassis has to be shortened by to fit the kit bodyshell.

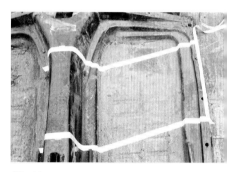

Masking tape is used to mark out the area to be cut. If the floorpan rear section is rusted or damaged, a 'tongue' can be left on the floorpan edge at the front part of the chevron so it slides into alignment to provide good metal for the floorpan corner when the halves are drawn together.

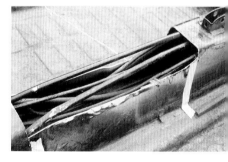

The top of the tunnel is carefully cut open first to access and break the conduit tack welds. The conduits run close to the tunnel top, and must not be damaged.

these will be reused. Two of these run close to the top of the tunnel and can be damaged easily. As the tunnel top

Once the thin floorpan centre sections have been cut, the tunnel has to be cut across the bottom. The floorpan semi-box section edges and remaining tunnel top are now all that hold the halves together, and are cut last.

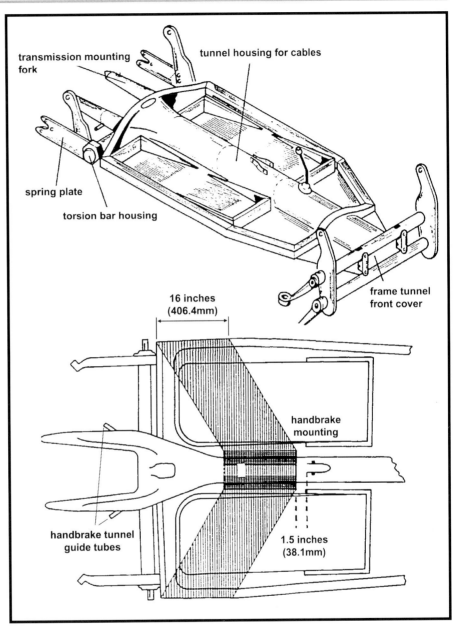

This diagram shows the 'chevron' cut that will be made across the chassis. This accommodates the taper at each side of the floorpan outer edge section, and gives a stronger weld. (Courtesy Cars & Car Conversions).

section is removed, it may be necessary to break the tack-welded tabs that fasten the cables to the tunnel. Unless heaters are to be used in the car, the heater cable guide tubes (front and back) can be cut. Finish cutting the floorpans ready to remove the chevron section. The metal of the floorpan is quite thin and can be cut with a sabre-saw, or a hacksaw. Cut inside the line that you have marked and then use tin-snips to trim the edge. Both right-hand and left-hand snips are available to make the job easier. Careful measuring will mean that there will be little hammering or grinding work to get the two halves to slide into alignment when the centre section is finally removed.

The underside of the tunnel is the area most often forgotten and it can easily be cut out with a hacksaw, again avoiding the control tubes. The chassis will have to be turned over to make this cut. The outside edge of the floorpans is only cut now, thus supporting the chassis while the longer cuts are made. The semi-box shape of the rear corners can be cut down slightly with a hacksaw for a nice clean edge (due to the chassis being wider at the rear) so that the front and rear halves can be slid into alignment.

Alternatively, if there is damage to the corners of the floorpan, a 'tongue' can be left on the forward part of the chassis so that it slides into place when the chassis is drawn together, and thus provides good metal for the corner of the floorpan.

The final cut is made on the centre tunnel with a hacksaw to cut out the remaining sections on each side below the opening that you have already made in the top of the tunnel. Before doing this, make sure that both halves of the chassis are fully sup-

Using a winch, the two halves are drawn together, and should require little hammer work to align everything if the initial measurements were accurate. The conduits are pushed out of the rear of the tunnel, and are then cut down.

ported, as there will then be nothing except the conduits holding them together. Once the cuts have been completed and the metal removed, use a small winch hooked onto strength members of each part of the chassis to pull it together, and carefully guide the control cable conduits out of the centre tunnel at the rear as you go. These can later be cut to size, and re-tack-welded into place. The rear corners are important for the overall alignment of the two sections, so trim these to fit as the halves finally meet.

If you have opted for the IRS rear section, then you will have to perform the operation on the two donor chassis, ensuring that the shape and profile of the two halves will meet accurately. Tunnel profiles vary, particularly between early king and link-pin chassis and the later IRS chassis. You may well find that the square-tunnel top of the IRS chassis will need a number of small cuts made into it to allow it to be heated and hammered down to match the rounded profile of the earlier chassis at the point where they meet to be welded. You will also have to feed the cable conduits of the torsion-bar chassis front into the rear section of the IRS floorpan as they are pulled

together, and locate them through their apertures in the rear of the chassis. The alternative is to cut the conduits accurately in each chassis half, and butt them together with an outer sleeve for support. As mentioned before, this is less satisfactory, as the cable ends may snag on the joint when inserted through the conduit.

Welding the chassis

If you do not have access to welding equipment or do not feel competent as a welder to re-weld the two halves back together, this is the point at which to bring in a specialist. With all the preparatory work done, this is a straightforward operation, and should not be overly expensive.

Use a few tack-welds to hold everything in place and then check alignment, squareness and lengthwise and diagonal measurement to ensure that the chassis does not have a twist in it before final welding. Clamp a length of tubing to the front framehead, and run two tape measures back to the rear suspension castings to ensure that the overall length of the chassis is the same on both sides. At

An IRS chassis rear section can be mated to the front section of an earlier chassis to provide different suspension combinations during the shortening process. Tunnel profiles may need to be re-worked to match accurately, and strengthened with strong metal plates after joining.

the same time, use a spirit level at the front and rear of the chassis to be sure that it isn't twisted.

If it's all square, complete the welding proper, working side to side and never in one spot for any length of time, to minimise the risk of distortion. Never attempt to weld in one go across the entire chassis. Again, don't forget the bottom of the tunnel. Re-check all measurements as you go, as misalignment will be difficult, if not impossible, to correct. Once all the welds are complete, and you have a unitary chassis, it is worthwhile making a few other modifications to strengthen the unit.

Modifying the shortened chassis

Small metal plates, about $1\frac{1}{2}$in, can be welded over the top of the long chevron joint, top and bottom, to prevent any chance of cracking and to add a lot of extra strength for just a few additional ounces of weight. The same is true across the tunnel top, where a wider plate can be used to bridge the joint. Seam sealer should always be used on all joints to prevent rust, prior to final painting.

Although the chassis is now considerably shorter and less prone to

An accurately shortened chassis, sandblasted, primered and seam-sealed at the joints ready for a top coat of paint. Always measure twice, and only cut once with chassis shortening! (Courtesy Chesil Motor Company).

chassis, and gives immense rigidity to the whole structure. Even jacking the complete car up at one corner will not cause any twist.

Whilst we are talking about strengthening the VW chassis, it is worthwhile mentioning front suspension stiffeners. Sold in pairs, these aftermarket parts replicate original VW parts, used to strengthen and support the torsion-bar front suspension. Made of heavy-wall steel tubing, the stiffeners clamp around the outer ends of the lower torsion-bar tube, and bolt to the front corners of the floorpan. Although primarily designed for off-road use, where the front suspension could be damaged by a heavy impact at the outer end of the suspension assembly, they are added insurance on any Beetle in the event of a front-end collision.

It is worth giving the chassis a final clean before applying a rust inhibitor/primer and final top-coat to finish the whole appearance of the buggy or kit-car underpinnings. For greater safety and strength in the open-topped buggy or kit-car, take the opportunity to also measure up for a full roll-cage with side impact protection, prior to the bodyshell being bolted in place.

Cables

The cables will also need shortening, and it is a good insurance policy to buy all new cables, and to take them to a specialist for shortening and to have the correct ends crimped on. For a chassis with a torsion-bar front and IRS rear, offer up all cables to the chassis and work out the exact amount by which the overall length has to shortened. This is simply because the handbrake location differs between VW models and years, and a mismatch on length will occur if the cables are simply shortened by the

A fully prepared and shortened Beetle chassis ready to accept its new kit bodyshell. This is a hybrid chassis made from the rear of an IRS 1303S Beetle, and the front of a disc braked 1500cc Beetle.

lex than stock, it is a good idea to stiffen the unit laterally by inserting and welding a heavy gauge 1in square box-section steel tubing into the external perimeter of the VW floorpans, once shaped to fit. The bolt holes will have to be redrilled through the new section, and longer bolts used to attach the new body, but this is a minor concession. The box-section

affords the same kind of strength as the stiffeners used by VW in the Cabriolet version of the Beetle. At the rear corners of the floorpans, a similar weight tube should be bent to fit underneath the chassis, and welded to the lateral reinforcement at the corner of the pans and also to the central tunnel. This provides a brace that effectively 'cantilevers' under the

EMPI front suspension stiffeners protect the outer ends of the lower torsion-bar tube from accidental damage.

same amount as the overall chassis length. If you are fitting the Porsche 944 rear disc brake system, the handbrake cables will also have to be modified, as detailed in the last chapter.

SWING-AXLE TO IRS CONVERSION

Owners of swing-axle rear suspension Beetles who wish to uprate their vehicles to the vastly superior IRS can do so by welding the mounts for the IRS diagonal arms to the rear frame forks and torsion housing assembly on the earlier chassis. This is a job that can only be recommended with the body removed, as there would not be enough room to work underneath a full-bodied sedan.

It will be necessary to find a pair of the IRS mounts from a scrapped VW Type 3 (which are more easily accessible on the torsion-bar housing than the Beetle, since they do not abutt a chassis frame horn), or to buy aftermarket brackets made by companies such as Chenowth to make the

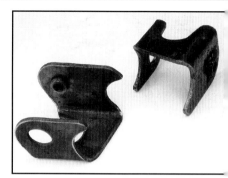

To convert a swing-axle Beetle to the superior IRS design, mounts will have to be added to the rear frame forks and torsion housing assembly. Chenworth mounts (US), or those from a scrapped Type 3 are required.

conversion. You will also need: the IRS gearbox itself; the diagonal A-arm assemblies; the locating Allen bolts and spacers which pass through the mount and act as a pivot; stub axles; driveshafts and driveshaft bolts and spreader plates; constant velocity joints; spring-plates; torsion-bars and covers. Finding the parts from a Super Beetle in the breaker's yard will be the best source, though you may also wish to substitute some of these parts for the Porsche 944 items we have already looked at. Dependant on the year of the parts sourced, the nose cone of the IRS gearbox may also have to be exchanged with that from the original swing-axle gearbox to enable it to fit the pre-1973 type of front transmission mounting.

Before disassembling the parts from the IRS donor chassis, make sure that the position of the spring-plates relative to the A-arms is marked with a single scribe mark, as these parts will need to go back together in perfect alignment once transplanted onto the earlier chassis. The bolts which hold

Front stiffeners fitted to the front suspension of a high performance Beetle. (Courtesy Mike Key).

he spring-plates to the A-arms can
hen be removed. The A-arms them-
elves are released from the donor
chassis by undoing the large Allen bolt
which pivots the arm at the inner end,
with a large Allen key or gearbox drain
plug wrench. The A-arms can then be
removed together with the shock
absorbers. Take off the torsion-bar
end cover and carefully pull the
spring-plates off the torsion-bar, then
remove the rubber bushing inside the
housing. Since the torsion-bars will be
removed entirely from the housing,
mark the end in a way that will help
with future reassembly, i.e., left or
right-hand bar, position of vertical, etc.

If your original Beetle has five-
bolt brake drums and wheels, when
you come to refit them to the later
type of suspension, you will also need
to make a hardened metal spacer,
about $5/8$in wide, to fit between the
snout of the brake drum and the axle
nut. This is because the early brake
drums have a shorter profile than the
later four-bolt drums. However, this
will effectively give you less rear
braking power than on the equivalent
IRS setup, and the move to VW Type
3 drums or a rear disc conversion
should be considered. The IRS conversion provides the ideal opportunity
to uprate your rear brakes, and should
not be missed when the chassis is
being modified so much.

The swing-axle chassis needs to
be stripped of the gearbox, spring-
plates and torsion-bars. The most
obvious difference between the two
types of chassis are the flanges on the
outside of the frame horns where the
flexible and rigid brake lines meet and
are secured. These will require shortening by about 4in at the end that
joins the torsion housing. Cut around
the handbrake conduits which exit the
frame fork at each side and, by careful
and accurate work, you will still leave

New, replacement chassis manufactured by VW have the A-arm mount position marked on the chassis, but the mounts themselves are not fitted, and must be welded on.

the brake line mounts intact.

The next step is to measure
$10^{1}/4$in along the torsion-bar housing
from the inside of the side plate that
leads up to the shock absorber mounting (not the outer edge) and mark the
torsion tube at the horizontal centre.
Double-check that the chassis is level
and then position the new mount at a
20 degree upward angle and trace the
shape of the mount onto the torsion
tube and frame fork itself. This is the
shape that will have to be recessed
into the side of the frame fork. Allow
for the fact that the shape you mark
will be slightly oversize and, when
cutting, always keep inside the line.
On brand-new, replacement VW
Beetle chassis which are currently
available on the market, whilst the IRS
bracket is not fitted, the position is
marked on the side of the frame fork.
This, like all original swing-axle chassis, will still have to have the new
mount let into the side of the fork, but
it does provide an excellent

reference point.

A drill, a chisel and an assortment
of files will be required to get the hole
cut to the right size, but don't be
surprised if you take several attempts
at getting the mount to fit the hole,
and relieve the metal as necessary.
With the mount just placed in the hole
(but not welded), offer up the diagonal
A-arms which must be bolted up to
the fitted spring-plates to dictate the
inboard position of the mounting eyes.
This may well need some adjustment
to fit but should only be tack welded in
place when the mount is correctly
aligned. When both sides are tacked,
check that everything is level before
finally removing the arms, and welding
everything up. Always ensure that
weld is applied to either side of the
mount for a strong, safe and perma-
nent attachment. The A-arms can then
be permanently installed.

If, during the initial removal of the
flange at the side of the fork, the
handbrake conduit becomes dam-

aged, some 1/2in bore thin-wall steel tube will have to be sleeved onto the undamaged conduit and welded into place to effect a repair.

One final thing that will have to be considered when making this conversion is the profile of the top section of the rear chassis forks themselves. On an IRS Beetle, they are significantly flatter in profile than on a swing-axle car, to accommodate the constant velocity joints where they connect to the drive flanges. To re-profile the forks of the swing-axle chassis, the metal will have to be heated up with a blow-torch, and then hammered down into a similar shape. Using a transmission cradle bolted across the ends of the forks will minimise the risk of any unwanted distortion. The later IRS transmission can then be mounted onto the chassis using new urethane mounts, if desired, and attached to the axle shafts with CV joints at either end.

FRAME-HEAD SWAP

Although changing the front frame-head on a Beetle chassis is another example of serious surgery, there are a couple of circumstances in which it is entirely necessary. Firstly, the original frame-head on a torsion-bar suspension Beetle may be badly rusted, or even damaged due to misalignment caused by a minor frontal accident. Replacement will be the only answer to salvage the chassis and car in this case. The other instance is if an IRS Beetle chassis is to be reused beneath a swing-axle Beetle body, or a kit-car. Here, the MacPherson strut type of front suspension cannot be used as there is nowhere to locate the tops of the suspension towers. However, by completely removing the 'hammer-head' type front frame-head on the Super Beetle design, and replacing it

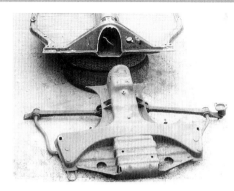

The Super Beetle chassis can be used as a basis for earlier Beetle or kit bodyshells if the original frame-head is changed to the earlier design. New, pattern, frame-heads are readily available.

with a conventional torsion-bar frame-head and torsion-bar suspension, the chassis then has the best of both worlds in the suspension department. One of the most widely accepted conversions in Beetle customising is to use an early bodyshell, but fitted to a late IRS floorpan to maximise the roadholding and performance of the vehicle.

It is always best to use a brand-new frame-head, rather than one sourced from another chassis. This is not just to use new metal when undertaking the replacement or conversion, but because replacement panels are made with an extra width and ridge to the tunnel section facing the front bulkhead, so that they slide over the existing tunnel for a better fit and greater strength. Measure the new panel against that fitted to the chassis before cutting anything, and allow for the additional measurement of the overlap piece on the new panel. The IRS frame-head, whilst different in shape where the suspension mounts, is the same as the earlier chassis at the point next to the bulkhead, and this is where the cut will have to be made. The central section of the tunnel underneath the chassis also differs slightly from the conventional torsion-

bar type, where it angles downwards slightly to form part of the 'hammer-head'. The mismatch created by attaching the earlier type of frame-head will require a shaped plate to be fabricated from flat steel to join this gap.

A hacksaw, or a mechanical sabre saw with a fine cutting blade will be needed to cut away the old frame-head, and the edge de-burred. If the original petrol pipe is still located within the tunnel, this can either be retained, if in good condition, or cut away and a new one laid into the car, running down the side of the central tunnel. Offer the new frame-head up to the truncated chassis, and check the measurements and alignment of the panel. A little grinding and hammering will normally be required to get the two sections perfectly aligned.

Put a few tack-welds on each side, just to hold things together, and then measure the chassis diagonally from the right front corner to the left rear, and vice versa. As with shortening a chassis, clamp a tube across the front of the frame-head in the position of one of the torsion tubes, and place a level on it. Only if it is even, and the diagonal measurements are exact can the two be finally welded together top and bottom, using seam welds for

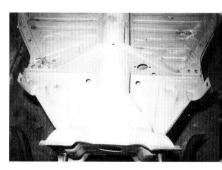

The new frame-head has an overlapping flange that allows the panel to fit over the front part of the cut tunnel section, and to be welded along each seam for maximum strength.

strength. All the welds should have a coat of seam sealer brushed on to them before finally painting the panel to provide some weather protection.

BEETLE CABLES AND PEDAL ASSEMBLIES

With many Beetles that are still on the road being nearly 30 years old (and some more than that), it's inevitable that parts wear out and things break. Whilst the chassis of your Beetle is receiving an overhaul with the more glamorous parts, such as disc brakes and suspension adjusters, it is worth checking and replacing the operating cables that run within conduits through the central tunnel.

Accelerator cables

Starting with the accelerator, there really couldn't be an easier cable to change on the Beetle than this. At the engine end, the cable attaches to a small clamp screw or nut on the carburettor lever. This is easily undone with a screwdriver or ring spanner (depending on the year). The cable travels through the centre tunnel in its conduit and exits at the pedal end with one of two arrangements: either an eye on the end of the cable which is attached to the accelerator lever by a clevis pin and split pin, or a shaped endpiece which locates directly into the accelerator lever.

On right-hand-drive cars, the accelerator lever itself is hidden behind a side cover bolted to the tunnel which is located under a metal foot-plate beneath the front floor-mat. On left-hand-drive cars, the cable can easily be seen where it attaches to the accelerator pedal. The cable is therefore simply pulled out at the front end and a new (well-greased) cable replaces it, being routed through the conduit in the tunnel to the rear of the chassis. A smaller metal conduit passes through the engine fan-housing to direct the cable up to the mounting at the side of the carburettor. The only upgrade possible with this cable is to install a heavy-duty $1/8$in racing accelerator cable instead. These are virtually indestructible, and will outlive any road-going Beetle.

Handbrake cables

Replacement of the two handbrake cables has been detailed in the section on rear suspension, since their removal requires the disassembly of the rear brake drums from the axles to access their eye mountings on the operating levers. The threaded ends of the handbrake cables are mounted to the ratchet operated handbrake lever inside the car, where it is mounted between the two front seats on the top of the central tunnel. The mounting plate or collars for the handbrake cables is hidden beneath a rubber boot, which prevents dirt collecting on the pivot points for the handbrake, and the cable ends. The boot, incidentally, tends to perish and split with old age, and can be changed for a new one after changing the cables. Replacements come in original black material, or numerous colours, if you

Handbrake cables are mounted to the handbrake lever, and are hidden by a rubber boot. The control levers that operate the Beetle heating system are attached to the same mount which provides the handbrake lever location.

wish to coordinate their appearance throughout the Beetle.

Heater cables

Whilst we are looking at the handbrake assembly, it's worth checking out the cables that operate the heater system in the car. These mount at either side of the handbrake (except on the early cars where a regulator sleeve and knob was employed) and are operated by a pull lever. One lever operates the two short cables that open vents below the rear seat, the other attaches to the two 'long' cables that open the flap controls of the heat exchangers, thus allowing hot air to enter the car's interior. The cable ends fit through small clamps on the control operating levers which are prone to rusting and subsequent failure in operation. If heater efficiency in the car drops, this is the first thing to check.

Replacement of either set of cables is very straightforward and consists of undoing the clamp mounting at the heat exchanger end or under the rear seat, and removal of the operating lever which is mounted at the side of the handbrake housing. A single nut is all that holds the lever on and, once undone, the lever can be prised off its locating pin and pulled forward together with the cables. Do not lose the positioning of the washer and retaining plate when the lever is removed, but otherwise it's an easy job. Grease the new cables to protect them from rust and to ensure smoothness in operation. Where the cables exit the end of the frame fork to run towards the operating levers on the heat exchangers, there should be a small rubber sleeve over the end of the conduit. It is frequently missing or perished, and should be replaced, as it prevents water entering the conduit and rusting the cable prematurely.

Clutch cable and pedal assembly

The Beetle pedal assembly is a very functional unit, combining the clutch, brake and accelerator pedals in a floor-mounted position. Unlike most modern vehicles with pendulum-type clusters, the Beetle arrangement – which was also used on some early Porsche models – has one major drawback. Dirt, and other deposits transported into the car via the driver's feet, tends to collect around the base of the cluster and impairs the free movement of the pedals.

It is a good idea to overhaul the whole cluster at a time when other maintenance work is being carried out, and the obvious opportunity is during replacement of the clutch cable. The cable itself runs in a conduit within the central tunnel, and passes through a

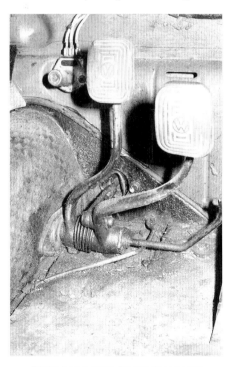

Right-hand-drive Beetle foot pedal assembly consisting of the accelerator pedal (far right), footbrake (centre), and clutch pedal (left). The assembly must be removed to access the clutch cable.

flexible guide tube located on to a boss attached to the gearbox at the back end of the chassis. This flexible tube is preloaded in a downward bow by about 1in to stop clutch judder and reduce strain on the cable. The threaded end of the cable passes through the eye of the clutch operating lever where it is held (and adjusted) by an adjusting nut and locknut on early cars, or a wing-nut on later cars.

At the front, the cable has an eye in the solid end that is crimped on to it. This locates over a hook on the operating shaft of the clutch pedal, and is situated on the left-hand side of the tunnel regardless of whether the vehicle is left or right-hand drive. The pedal clusters of the left and right-hand Beetles are, of necessity, different in their design due to their location in the car. We will look at that of the right-hand-drive Beetle, simply because this takes the most work to disassemble and rebuild, though the underlying principles are the same for both. In both cases, a workshop manual will provide good cross-section views of the parts and fittings for precise reference.

To save hitting your head on the steering wheel whilst working on the cluster, it is a good idea to remove the front seats and give yourself the maximum area in which to work. Remove the rubber floormats and passenger footplate, which partially cover the accelerator cable housing. Next, remove the two bolts that hold the cover to the side of the transmission tunnel. With this placed to one side, the accelerator cable and actuating arm are exposed. Carefully remove the circlip from the operating shaft and then the arm itself. The cable can remain in position unless it needs replacing as part of the general overhaul. Don't be surprised if the cover plate that forms the mounting for the

accelerator actuating arm won't slide off the pedal inner shaft without the application of releasing fluid and some gentle persuasion.

Moving to the driver's side of the tunnel, remove the accelerator pedal from its floor mount and off the linkage that pivots on the end of the operating shaft. Make sure that you keep a note of where all the disassembled pieces go, ready for when rebuild time arrives, as there are plenty of loose parts to remember.

It is easier to undo the clutch cable from its mounting through the operating arm at the rear of the car before you unbolt the pedal cluster from the floor. With this removed it is then necessary to disconnect the piston pushrod of the brake master-cylinder. On older Beetles, this is fixed to the brake pedal by a pin and circlip which, being an interference fit, takes some force with a drift to knock out. Later cars have a strong circlip that attaches the eye of the pushrod to the pedal and also locates the pedal return spring.

The bolts securing the cluster to the floor can then be undone. They locate a metal plate to the floor that acts as a 'stop' for the pedals when at rest, as well as mounting the outer end of the pedal shaft to the top of the plate itself. The position of both should be marked before finally working the whole pedal cluster out from the central tunnel, once the clutch cable disengages from its hook on the clutch pedal shaft. The whole unit can then be taken to a workbench for full disassembly. Using circlip pliers, the circlips at each end of the shaft can be removed to allow the two pedals to slide off. Remove the long accelerator shaft from the main outer shaft, and clean and lubricate the parts so they will give a smooth operating motion when reassembled.

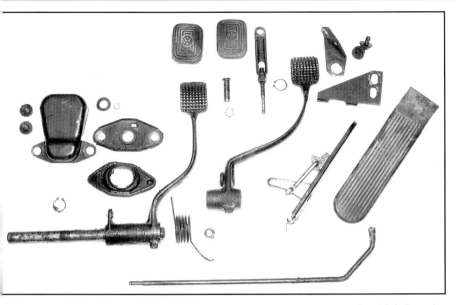

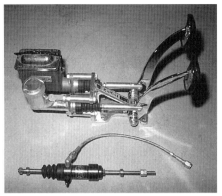

The high performance Neal pedal assembly uses an hydraulic clutch with a slave cylinder for smoother and longer-lasting operation. The unit will fit a Beetle sedan with minimum bulkhead clearancing.

Disassembled Beetle pedal components. These should all be cleaned and lubricated before being reassembled and refitted to the car.

Putting the cluster back together is a straightforward operation, using new circlips if any are broken or overstretched. The hardest part is fitting the new clutch cable and remounting the cluster to the floor. The new cable has to be greased and slid into the front end of the metal conduit within the tunnel, and the flexible guide tube at the rear of the chassis will need to be removed to allow the cable to be pushed through before being refitted.

With the cable through the tubing, the whole pedal cluster has to be set back in place with the clutch cable eye over the clutch pedal hook while the cluster is bolted back to the floor. The most successful way to attempt this operation is to put a loop of wire a few inches long through the cable eye so it can be pulled down on to the hook from outside the tunnel whilst pushing the cluster in to the tunnel. Once engaged, the wire can be pulled out and the unit bolted down to the floorpan. The stop plate may need minor adjustment to allow the faces of

the pedals to be set vertically, and the holes in the plate are of a slotted design to allow this adjustment. The clutch cable will then need adjusting at the threaded end attaching it to the operating arm, to give the correct clutch pedal free play which should not be less than $7/16$in or more than $13/16$in.

Hydraulic clutches
Whilst the stock clutch cable can be

A roller pedal can replace the original 'organ-pedal' accelerator, and gives greater throttle control. This design replicates the earliest type of VW Beetle accelerator pedal.

The Neal hydraulic pedal assembly, with custom made pedal covers, provides good looks and smooth operation in any Beetle or Beetle-based vehicle.

replaced, the high performance option is to dispense with it altogether, and replace it with an hydraulic clutch. These systems, available from a number of US manufacturers such as CNC, Jamar and Neal, consist of a complete clutch, brake and accelerator pedal assembly with integral fluid reservoirs supplying both brake and clutch systems. The clutch uses a slave cylinder that pulls the clutch operating arm, and mounts to the boss for the original guide tube on the transaxle side cover in place of the original cable.

Made essentially for custom-built

vehicles such as dune buggies and race cars, these pedal assemblies replace the entire VW assembly, and bolt to the floor, but do require the cutting of the Beetle front bulkhead panel to allow clearance for the integral fluid reservoirs. To minimise the amount of cutting Neal, in conjunction with Bernard Newbury in the UK, has developed a pedal assembly that can be installed in the Beetle with the minimum amount of work. The hydraulic assembly matches its brake system, and uses the hydraulic clutch slave cylinder for a smooth operation without reliance on the Beetle cable. Adjustment of free play of the slave unit is much the same as on a Beetle cable, with an adjusting nut on the end of the slave cylinder rod.

GEARSHIFTERS AND LOCKING SHIFTERS

For performance use, the stock Beetle gearshifter does not provide the best characteristics to make the most of other modifications that may have been made to the car, particularly in terms of the engine and transmission. It has a long 'throw' to the lever, and an unusual arrangement for the engagement of reverse gear – having to press down on the lever and slide it over towards the left side of the car before pulling it backwards.

Aftermarket suppliers have been quick to see the possibilities of enhancing the basic design, and there is now a wide range of performance shifters to choose from to improve your Beetle. Manufactured by US companies such as Bugpack, Gene Berg and EMPI, the essence of all the designs is twofold: to provide smoother gear selection whilst reducing the throw of the lever, and to improve the ease of reverse gear selection. The styles differ consider-

ably, and there is really no substitute for trying each of the designs (either on a company demonstrator car, or a friend's vehicle) to see which suits you, and the use of your Beetle.

The 'Hurst' style shifter, now made by EMPI, uses a shortened lever with a ball-top, but fitted with a 'trigger' style sliding section to the outside of the shaft which, when lifted, engages reverse as the lever is pulled backwards. The EMPI 'dual-handle' shifter has a 'T-handled' top, and a separate lever at the front with a smaller handle to pull it upwards and thus engage reverse. Bugpack, and similar aftermarket suppliers, have a short-throw lever with a push-button set into the handle. When depressed and the lever pulled back, reverse is selected.

The items made by Gene Berg utilise a similar system, and are very well-engineered. All come with fitting instructions that are very comprehensive. Berg also make a locking shifter

The Gene Berg shifter is a short-throw lever with a pushbutton to engage reverse. The forward-mounted button is wired to a brake 'line-lock' on this drag-racing Beetle.

which provides not only a superior gearchange, but added security for the vehicle. This item uses what is termed a 'Quickshift' baseplate as its mounting, and we will first take a look at the fitting of the Quickshift, and then a gear-lever lock.

The 'Quickshift' kit

The Quickshift kit is designed to reduce the stock Beetle gearlever movement by 40%, and makes the gear-changing less of a chore. The kit comes in four parts: a baseplate for the gear lever housing, a rounded block that fits over the lever itself, and two long threaded bolts. Fitting is very straightforward, and consists of firstly unscrewing the gearlever knob, then removing the rubber gaiter that fits around the base of the lever (which can be replaced upon reassembly if it is split). With a 13mm spanner, undo the two bolts that hold the lever baseplate down onto the central tunnel. The spring underneath the plate will push it up, so work from side to side to avoid straining the components unnecessarily. Lift the lever away from the tunnel, but leave the separate, greased plate, incorporating the reverse gear lockout guide, in place. Put the Quickshift baseplate directly over this, and try not

The EMPI gearshift replicates the 'trigger' style Hurst shifter made in the 1960s & 1970s. The sliding shaft is lifted to engage reverse.

to lose the position of the reverse plate, as it can be adjusted slightly by moving it around.

Next, turn your attention to the lever. Slip it out from the metal baseplate and fit the rounded block over the top of the existing one. Grease this well and then refit the baseplate over it. Now simply fit the lever/baseplate over the Quickshift base, and use the longer bolts with the original washer to hold it all in place. Adjust the mechanism before finally tightening it down.

Gearshift locks

Gearshift locks are the ideal way to immobilise 6-volt Beetles which, obviously, do not have the 12-volt system required for most modern electrical security devices. They are also a visual deterrent to theft in an open-top vehicle such as the VW Cabriolet or a dune buggy. In the 1960s, a German company called Sperwolf produced an original VW accessory that locked the gearlever in reverse or first, and was easy to install. A modern equivalent is the locking unit produced by Stateside company, West Coast Metric (WCM), which is an almost exact reproduction of the original item, apart from the absence of the ignition cutout that was a part of the earlier design.

Gene Berg also make locking versions of their standard and short-throw shifters, which are similar to the WCM item. The short-throw design

Gene Berg shifters come in several variants, such as this design, to complement their five-speed Beetle gearbox. The unit also provides a locking mechanism.

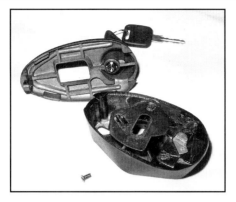

West Coast Metric (WCM) makes a gear lock to help prevent Beetle theft. The design locks the vehicle in gear, and cannot be bypassed like an electrical immobiliser. It is ideally suited to cars with a six-volt electrical system.

sits on top of a Quickshift spacer plate to achieve the short throw required.

Both manufacturers' units are neat looking and compact items, featuring an opening in the top for the gearlever to exit from, and a key lock mounted at the front end. The Gene Berg shifter has the advantage of having a button-activated reverse selection, and a shorter throw due to the installation of the Quickshift plate, but is a bulkier unit. The WCM unit is cheaper, more compact, and less obtrusive, so again, it is worth examining and trying both before you buy.

It is the WCM unit that is illustrated here, but the same principles apply to both, and instructions are supplied with each, in any case. The first job is to remove the screw on the end of the unit, and turn the key sideways so that the body of the unit can be slid apart into a top and bottom half. Make a mental note of where all the internal components sit, or make a diagram of them, because it

is necessary to remove and refit them.

There are two sliding plates, pivoted on one side, held by a small spring inserted between them and with an elongated slot in the middle through which the gearlever sits. At the front end, there are two moving pins – one to fit into and lock the sliding plates, and the other a grooved piece that matches the key lock and turns with the rotation of the key. Fitting the unit to the Beetle requires the removal of the two bolts that hold the plate of the VW gearlever. The plate can then be removed, but the spring should be left in place. The shaped metal plate that sits on top of the central tunnel and provides the location for the gears will stay in place beneath the spring, and should not be disturbed. The gearlever itself also stays in place.

The base section of the new locking unit is then placed over the gear-lever, the spring, and the selector plate, and is secured with the two bolts. Before finally tightening the bolts down, it is worthwhile sliding this back and forth slightly to make sure that it seats down correctly on the spring and plate. Try to select all of the gears to ensure all the components have seated correctly, and adjust the relationship of the base unit to the plate and gearlever to suit.

Slip the two sliding plates over the gearlever and locate them on the left-hand pin. Tighten them up with the small spring that locates between them at the rear. Looking at the two front pins, these now have to mate up to the lock unit in the top of the case when it is rested on top. Turn the key sideways in the top half of the lock, offer it up to the base, and slide it backwards into the positioning groove until it can go no further. Whilst fitting the top, the key should remain turned sideways, otherwise you will not be able to extract the key from the unit once the gearlever is locked in position.

To complete the job, fit the end screw that holds the top and bottom halves together, and put a new rubber boot around the lever base to stop dirt falling into the lock and gear lever mechanisms. The locked unit is effective, can't be bypassed or switched off like an electronic alarm, and is cheap insurance for any Beetle.

CONCLUSION

There will always be new high performance and aftermarket parts coming on to the ever-expanding market for Beetle-related products. Many of these will be reviewed in the Beetle and VW magazines that are available, and you will have to decide for yourself if they offer you the type of features that will benefit your vehicle, and are within your price range. If they appear to suit your needs, always obtain as much information about them, and whether they will need other parts to make them fit or work on the car. If possible, talk to other owners/drivers who have used them and can recommend them. You may learn a lot before you start spending your hard-earned cash!

Visit Veloce on the Web - www.veloce.co.uk

NOTES

Appendix 1
Suppliers

Autocavan Components Ltd., 103 Lower Weybourne Lane, Badshot Lea, Farnham, Surrey, GU9 9LG, UK - *Aftermarket and performance parts; disc brake conversions; lowered suspensions; narrowed axles.*

Bernard Newbury, 1 Station Road, Leigh-on-Sea, Essex, SS9 1ST, UK - *Neal disc brake conversions; Hurst and Gene Berg shifters.*

Big Boys Toys, 13 Breach Road, W. Thurrock, Essex, RM20 3NR, UK - *Aftermarket parts; suspension components; CB Performance dropped spindles.*

Chesil Motor Company, Cogden, Burton Bradstock, Bridport, Dorset, DT6 4RN ,UK - *VW chassis shortening; Speedster kits.*

Custom & Speed Parts, Autoteile GmbH, Am Redder 3, 22941 Bargteheide, Germany - *Disc brake conversions; aftermarket and performance parts.*

Dave Palmer, Creative Engineering, The Old Chapel, The Street, East Knoyle, Wiltshire, SP3 6AJ, UK - *Custom & Speed Parts agent.*

German Car Co., Viscount House, Southend Airport, Southend, Essex, SS2 6YL, UK - *Aftermarket and performance parts; disc brake conversions; dropped spindles; Bugpack parts.*

GT Mouldings, PO Box 966, Portslade, Brighton, BN41 2GL, UK - *Shortened chassis and dune buggy kits.*

John Maher Racing, Unit 16, Albany Road Industrial Estate, Chorlton, Manchester, M21 0AZ, UK - *Performance suspensions and engines.*

Kingfisher Kustoms, Unit 5, Oldbury Road, Smethwick, W. Midlands, B66 1NU, UK - *Chassis shortening; aftermarket parts; suspension components; disc brake kits.*

Performance Ghia, http:// <http://www> performanceghia.webjump.com. *Web site for Porsche brake conversions, and performance VW information.*

Red 9 Design, 10 Jasmine Walk, Evesham, Worcestershire, WR11 6AL, UK - *Lowered spring-plates.*

Spectra Dynamics Ltd., Unit 1A, Ffordd Derwen Industrial Estate, Rhyl ,Denbighshire, LL18 2YR, UK - *Polyurethane replacement bushes.*

Speedy Cables (London) Ltd., The Mews, St. Paul Street, Islington, London, N1 7BU, UK - *Cable shortening.*

Superflex Ltd., Meadow View, Farthing Green Lane, Stoke Poges, Slough, SL2 4JH, UK - *Polyurethane replacement bushes.*

VW Discount, Heussner & Stauber, Hannoversche Strasse 41, 34355 Staufenberg, Landwehrhagen, Germany - *Ventilated and crossed-drilled disc conversion for Beetle stub-axles and Porsche calipers.*

Wizard Roadsters, 41 Eton Wick Road, Eton Wick, Slough, SL4 6PJ, UK - *Aftermarket parts; brake parts; lowered front suspensions.*

WSB Buggy, P.O. Box 1118, D-65358, Geisenheim, Germany, www.wsb-buggy.de - *Dune buggy kits.*

US SUPPLIERS

CB Performance Products Inc., 1715 N. Farmersville Boulevard, Farmersville, CA 93223, USA - *Dropped spindles; disc brake kits.*

CNC Inc., 1221 West Morena Boulevard, San Diego, CA 92110, USA - *Disc brake conversions.*

Dee Engineering Inc., 3560 Cadillac Ave., Costa Mesa, CA 92626, USA - *Bugpack aftermarket and performance parts; suspensions and brakes.*

Gene Berg Enterprises, 1725 N. Lime Street, Orange, CA 92865, USA - *Avis adjusters; caster shims.*

Kymco, 2121 Harbour, Costa Mesa, California, CA 92627, USA - *Torque-Meister tool; disc brake conversions; front suspensions.*

Summers Brothers, 530 S. Mountain Ave., Ontario, CA 91762, USA - *Heavy-duty spring plates and off-road components.*

NOTES

Appendix 2
Chassis numbers & transmission codes

IRS (INDEPENDENT REAR SUSPENSION

The term 'IRS' is the term used in this book to indicate those models fitted with the two CV-jointed driveshafts, and diagonal A-arms, on each side of the gearbox. As explained in the text, the term 'IRS' is a misnomer, as all Beetles are, strictly speaking, fitted with independent rear suspensions, even on the swing-axle cars.

However, the term has become the accepted description of the later type of rear suspension system, and is therefore refered to as such throughout this book.

VW BEETLE CHASSIS NUMBERS 1940 – 1986

From 1940 to 1959, VW Beetle chassis numbers were listed January – December. For 1960 only, numbers were listed from January to July.

Prior to1960, Volkswagen did not utilise a model year system except in the USA, where 'model year' tended to correspond with the calendar year dates, but was modified by shipment batch dates.

From 1st August 1960, major production changes were reserved for the start of a new model year, starting in August of each year. This process of making significant changes at the start of a new model year was only introduced in 1960 since, prior to August of that year, all changes to Beetles were made progressively.

Thus 1st August 1960 marks the start of the 1961 model year; 1st August 1961 marks the start of the 1962 model year and so on.

When ordering parts, always quote the exact chassis number to avoid problems especially in relation to vehicles made before August 1960.

VW BEETLE CHASSIS NUMBERS 1940 – 1968

Year	Chassis Numbers
1940	1 - 00 001 to 1 - 01 000
1941	1 - 01 001 to 1 - 05 656
1942	1 - 05 657 to 1 - 014 383
1943	1 - 014 384 to 1 - 032 302
1944	1 - 032 303 to 1 - 051 999
1945	1 - 052 000 to 1 - 053 814
1946	1 - 053 815 to 1 - 063 796
1947	1 - 063 797 to 1 - 072 743
1948	1 - 072 744 to 1 - 091 921
1949	1 - 091 922 to 1 - 0138 554
1950	1 - 0138 555 to 1 - 0220 133
1951	1 - 0220 134 to 1 - 0313 829
1952	1 - 0313 830 to 1 - 0428 156
1953	1 - 0428 157 to 1 - 0579 682
1954	1 - 0579 683 to 1 - 0781 884
1955	1 - 0781 885 to 1 - 1 060 929
1956	1 - 1 060 930 to 1 - 1 394 119
1957	1 394 120 to 1 774 680 (Type '1' prefix then dropped)
1958	1 774 681 to 2 226 206
1959	2 226 207 to 2 801 613
1960	2 801 614 to 3 192 506 (31st July 1960)
1961	3 192 507 to 4 010 994 (start of new 1st August – 31st July model year system)
1962	4 010 995 to 4 846 835
1963	4 846 836 to 5 677 118
1964	5 677 119 to 6 502 399
1965	115 000 001 to 115 979 200 (start of 9-digit numbering)
1966	116 000 001 to 116 1021 298
1967	117 000 001 to 117 844 892
1968	118 000 001 to 118 1016 098

VW BEETLE CHASSIS NUMBERS 1969 – 1986

1969 .... 119 000 001 to 119 1093 704
1970 .... 110 2000 001 to 110 3095 945
    (start of 10-digit numbering)
1971 .... 111 2000 001 to 111 3143 119
1972 .... 112 2000 001 to 112 2961 362
1973 .... 113 2000 001 to 113 3021 911
1974 .... 114 2000 001 to 114 2828 457
1975 .... 115 2000 001 to 115 2266 092
1976 .... 116 2000 001 to 116 2176 287
1977 .... 117 2000 001 to 117 2096 890
1978   118 2000 001 to 118 ???? ???
    (Beetle sedan production ceased in Germany in January 1978, but continued in Mexico, in Brazil until July 1996, and in SouthAfrica until January 1979. The last chassis number for 1978 is either a 1303 Cabriolet, a Mexican 1200L in July 1979, or even a South African model)
1979 .... 119 2000 001 to 119 2121 136
1980 .... 11A 000 001 to 11A 0020 000
    (German 1303 Cabriolet production finishes at chassis number: 1592 044 140)
    VW moves to standardisation of international Vehicle Identification Numbers (VIN) numbers.
1981 .... 11B 000 001 to 11B 013 340
    (Production in Puebla, Mexico)
1982 .... 11CM 000 001 to 11C 009 836
1983 .... 11DM 000 001 to 11D 017 323
1984 .... 11EM 000 001 to 11E 020 000
1985 .... 11FM 000 001 to 11F 020 000
1986 .... 11GM 000 001 to 11G 003 213
Thereafter, each year begins '11' followed by a letter and 'M'

TRANSMISSION CODES

AA	1200	4.375	From chassis No. 0981 810
AB	1300	4.375	up to 8/70
AC	1500	4.125	Also some 1300 from 8/70
AD	1200	4.375	Limited Slip Differential (LSD)
AE	1300	4.375	- with LSD
AF	1500	4.125	LSD up to 8/70; also some 1300 from 8/70
AG	1200	4.375	Type 147 (Fridolin)
AH	1500	4.125	IRS from 8/68
	1600	4.125	8/69 - 8/72
AK	1500	3.875	Type 181 up to 8/70
	1600	3.875	Type 181 from 8/70
AL	1500	3.875	Type 181 with LSD up to 8/70
	1600	3.875	Type 181 with LSD from 8/70 (the 181 model – known as the 'Trekker' in Britain - was fitted with swing axles and reduction gears. The US counterpart – known as the 'Thing' – had IRS rear suspension.
AM	1300	4.375	Saloon and Cabriolet from 8/70
AN	1600	3.875	KG with IRS from 8/70
AO	1600	3.875	KG from 8/70
AP	1300	4.375	LSD from 8/70
AQ	1600	4.125	LSD 8/70 - 8/72
AR	1600	3.875	KG with LSD from 8/70
AS	1600	3.875	Type 1 from 8/72
AT	1600	3.875	1303s and Cabriolet from 8/72
AU	1600	3.875	- with LSD
BA	1300/1500	4.375	Semi-auto from 8/68 - 8/70
BC	1300/1500	4.375	- with LSD
BE	1600	4.125	Semi-auto from 8/70 - 8/71
BF	1600	4.125	- with LSD
BG	1300	4.125	KG with Semi-auto from 8/70
BH	1300	4.125	- with LSD
BJ	1300	4.375	Semi-auto from 8/70
BK	1300	4.375	- with LSD
DA	1500/1600	4.125	Type 3 swingaxle up to 8/68*
DB	1500/1600	4.125	- with LSD*
DC	1500/1600	4.125	Type 3 with IRS from 8/68
DD	1500/1600	4.125	- with LSD

Note. The reinforced swingaxle design was available on post - 8/64 VW Type 3 models (Type 36) as an option (M263)

Glossary of terms

ENGLISH	AMERICAN
Accelerator	Gas pedal
Anti-roll bar	Stabiliser or sway bar
Bonnet	Front hood
Bulkhead	Firewall
Bush	Bushing
Circlip	Snap-ring
Clearance	Lash
Damper	Shock absorber
Disc	Rotor/disk
Drop arm	Pitman arm
Gearbox	Transmission
Gearchange	Shift
Halfshaft/driveshaft	Axle shaft
Handbrake	Parking brake
Leading shoe	Primary shoe
Petrol	Gasoline
Petrol tank	Gas tank
Seized	Frozen
Spanner	Wrench
Split pin	Cotter pin
Steering arm	Spindle arm
Swarf	Metal chips
Trackrod	Tie-rod
Trailing shoe	Secondary shoe
Transmission	Whole driveline
Tyre	Tire
Vice	Vise
Wheel nut	Lug nut
Wing	Fender

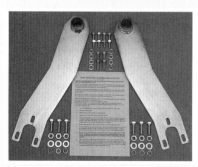

113

The new BERG Catalog is in stock and available for purchase. Call and order yours today! 160 pages of information simply not available anywhere else. Also get gb801-set mandatory reading for the serious vw enthusiast

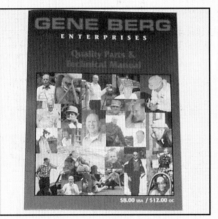

Why is it that 'economical' used to mean thrifty or long lasting and now it means stripped to the bone or that the company has cut every corner possible to pass this part on to you as cheap as they possibly can?
Buy Genuine GBE products where economical still means thrifty and long lasting

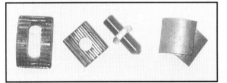

Avis Front End Adjusters
The Avis adjuster. Works for both link pin and ball joint. To maintain soft ride install in both beams. For stiff ride install one in the bottom beam only. Has about a 4" adjustment.
Complete with Berg copyrighted instructions. Front end alignment required before driving the car. Sold per each.
GB 690........................Avis adjuster.

Front Axle Beam with Adjusters
VWA113401021AL.........Link pin beam with adjusters.
VWA113401021DL.......Ball joint beam with adjusters.

Caster Wedges

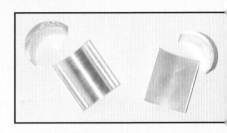

Caster wedges have been used by VW from the early 50's for cars that wandered in the wind or did not have enough caster from the factory. At least one set was a must if the car was to be driven over 75 MPH. Some cars are manufactured by VW that may have the minimum allowable caster. What this does is allows the car to wander as the speed gets higher or more than normal in a crosswind.
People that lower the front end of their car, raise the rear end, or both, will aggravate this situation even more. I have seen lowered cars that were almost impossible to keep in one lane at 60 MPH. Some vehicles require more than one caster wedge just to get back to stock and even more to make it safe at 100 MPH. You may need one set of our 3.4 degree and one set of our 1.5 degree. This all depends on the amount of lowering and the maximum speed the car will reach. By adding the proper amount of caster wedges, you tip the beam out at the bottom and increase the caster to eliminate wandering. It is impossible for anyone to guess what "your" car needs. We strongly recommended that the caster be checked before ordering to determine what you actually need.
For more information on front and rear suspension see GB 801-SUSPENSION specifically for drag racing or fast street cars. Made in USA by GBE.

Note: 1 One set of 2 is required for a front end unless you are adding wheel stagger to one side or correcting for a bent frame horn.
Note: 2 GB 681 caster wedges that are 1.5 degrees are about 3.8mm thick and use the factory 90mm bolt. 3.4 degrees are about 8.6mm thick and use GB 681B 100mm long bolts. We also offer 110mm for applications that require stacking more caster wedges. You can calculate what you need by these measurements.
Note: Shims can be stacked to achieve desired caster.

A Needle In A Hay Stack
For those of you that have read our (GB 801-TRANS) article about proper building of the VW gearbox for high performance applications and have been one of the flood of people that has called trying to find the needle bearings to perform the hand pack operation, we have finally found them. For those of you that have not read the article, a little background may bring you into focus. One of the things that provide much longer first and second gear life (also 3rd/4th) under high HP loads is to hand pack the needle bearings, providing more bearing surface area. In other words, install individual (single) needle bearings rather than a caged unit. This provides many more needles to keep the gear from pushing away or tipping (cocking) in relationship to the mainshaft gear, which can prematurely cause breakage. For complete details you **MUST** read GB 801-TRANS and I can assure you all of my technical articles are extremely valuable for every VW owner and mechanic.
In the past it was necessary to remove extra needle bearings from the 1961 through 1963 transaxles to use for this operation. Because more than twice as many needles are needed, it requires disassembly of three gear boxes to get enough needle bearings for building one high performance gear box. So, why not just buy the replacement caged needle bearings from VW or an aftermarket supplier? The reason is the caged needle bearings required have been superseded by VW with a shorter one that comes in a plastic cage and it cannot be used. For years we have looked for a supplier of just the single needle bearings that were the correct length without the cage so we would not need to find core gearboxes to acquire the needed parts nor would we have to make spacers. These are made to the proper length to fit the gears. Well, at long last we have succeeded in finding a supplier that can get them for me. Originated by Ray Vallero and updated by Gene Berg in 1980.

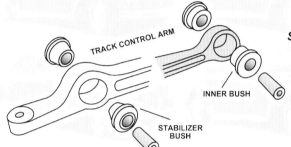
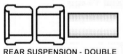

Manta-Ray

- 2+2 seating
- Short wheelbase
- Fits VW Beetle chassis shortened 16"
- Hand laminated glassfibre

G.T. MOULDINGS
MANTA RAY

Renegade

- Self coloured bodyshell
- 2+2 seating
- Short wheelbase
- Fits VW Beetle chassis shortened 14½"

G.T. MOULDINGS
Renegade

Britain's best buggies

- Buggy kits in short or long wheelbase
- Buggy side panels, bonnets, dashboards and seat shells
- Polished alloy windscreen frames
- Chrome headlamps and lighting equipment
- Pulley guards, fan shrouds and battery boxes

GT Mouldings, PO Box 966, Portslade, Brighton BN41 2GL UK. Tel: +44(0)1273 430505
For full details send a stamped SAE. Foreign enquiries send 2 x IRCs.

ALSO FROM VELOCE PUBLISHING -

HOW TO BUILD & MODIFY SPORTSCAR & KIT CAR SUSPENSION & BRAKES
by Des Hammill

ISBN 1 901295 08 7
Price £14.99*

A book in the *SpeedPro* series.

• Applies to all two seater sportscars and kit cars with wishbone front suspension, coil springs, telescopic shock absorbers and wishbone or trailing arm rear suspension.
• Basic information applies to all cars.
• Written in a clear understandable style with over 100 detailed original diagrams.
• Cuts through the mystique and confusion surrounding suspension and handling improvements.
• Ideal for the home mechanic.
• Applies to road and track applications.
• Des Hammill is an engineer and a professional race car builder with many years of practical experience.

CONTENTS
Chassis integrity • Suspension geometry • Ride height • Negative camber, castor and Kingpin inclination • Springs and shock absorbers • Brakes • Setting up the car • Testing, alterations and adjustments • Index

SPECIFICATION
Paperback. 250 x 207mm (portrait). 112 pages. Over 100 detailed original diagrams.

RETAIL SALES
Veloce books are stocked by or can be ordered from bookshops and specialist mail order companies. In case of difficulty we can supply direct (credit cards accepted).

* Price subject to change.

Veloce Publishing Plc, 33 Trinity Street, Dorchester, Dorset DT1 1TT, England. Tel: 01305 260068/ Fax: 01305 268864/E-mail: veloce@veloce.co.uk

Visit Veloce on the Web - www.veloce.co.uk

ALSO FROM VELOCE PUBLISHING -

HOW TO BUILD & POWER TUNE DISTRIBUTOR-TYPE IGNITION SYSTEMS
by Des Hammill

ISBN 1 874105 76 6
Price £10.99*

A book in the *SpeedPro* series.

Expert practical advice from an experienced race engine builder on how to build an ignition system that delivers maximum power reliably. A lot of rubbish is talked about ignition systems and there's a bewildering choice of expensive aftermarket parts which all claim to deliver more power. Des Hammill cuts through the myth and hyperbole and tells readers what *really* works, so that they can build an excellent system without wasting money on parts and systems that simply don't deliver.

Ignition timing and advance curves for modified engines is another minefield for the inexperienced, but Des uses his expert knowledge to tell readers how to optimise the ignition timing of *any* high-performance engine.

The book applies to all four-stroke gasoline/petrol engines with distributor-type ignition systems, including those using electronic ignition modules: it does not cover engines controlled by ECUs (electronic control units).

CONTENTS
Why modified engines need more idle speed advance • Static idle speed advance setting • Estimating total advance settings • Vacuum advance • Ignition timing marks • Distributor basics • Altering rate of advance • Setting total advance • Quality of spark •

THE AUTHOR
Des Hammill has a background in precision engineering and considers his ability to work very accurately a prime asset. Des has vast experience of building racing engines on a professional basis. Having lived and worked in many countries around the world, he currently splits his time between the UK and New Zealand.

SPECIFICATION
Softback • 250 x 207mm (portrait) • 64 pages • Over 70 black & white photographs and line illustrations.

RETAIL SALES
Veloce books are stocked by or can be ordered from bookshops and specialist mail order companies. Alternatively, Veloce can supply direct (credit cards accepted).

* Price subject to change.

Veloce Publishing Plc, 33 Trinity Street, Dorchester, Dorset DT1 1TT, England. Tel: 01305 260068/ Fax: 01305 268864/E-mail: veloce@veloce.co.uk

ALSO FROM VELOCE PUBLISHING -

HOW TO CHOOSE CAMSHAFTS & TIME THEM FOR MAXIMUM POWER
by Des Hammill

ISBN 1 901295 19 2
Price £10.99*

A book in the **SpeedPro** series.

Explains in simple language how to choose the right camshaft/s for *YOUR* application and how to find the camshaft timing which gives maximum performance.
• Also explained are all aspects of camshaft design and the importance of lobe phasing, duration & lift.
• Applies to all 4-stroke car-type engines with 4, 5, 6 or 8 cylinders.
• Des Hammill is an engineer and a professional race engine builder with many years of experience.
• Avoids wasting money on modifications that don't work.
• Applies to road and track applications.

CONTENTS
Introduction • Using This Book &
Essential Information • Chapter 1: Terminology • Chapter 2: Choosing the Right Amount of Duration • Chapter 3: Checking Camshafts • Chapter 4: Camshaft Timing Principles • Chapter 5: Camshaft Problems • Chapter 6: Timing Procedure - Cam-in-Block Engines • Chapter 7: Camshaft Timing Procedure - S.O.H.C. Engines • Chapter 8: Camshaft Timing Procedure - T.O.H.C. Engines • Chapter 9: Engine Testing • Index.

THE AUTHOR
Des Hammill has a background in precision engineering and places great emphasis on accuracy. Des has vast experience of building all types of engine for many categories of motor racing. Having lived in many countries around the world, Des and his wife, Alison, currently live in Devon, England.

SPECIFICATION
Softback • 250 x 207mm (portrait) • 64 pages • 150 black & white photographs & line illustrations.

RETAIL SALES
Veloce books are stocked by or can be ordered from bookshops and specialist mail order companies. Alternatively, Veloce can supply direct (credit cards accepted).

* Price subject to change.

Veloce Publishing Plc, 33 Trinity Street, Dorchester, Dorset DT1 1TT, England. Tel: 01305 260068/ Fax: 01305 268864/E-mail: veloce@veloce.co.uk

ALSO FROM VELOCE PUBLISHING -

HOW TO BUILD & POWER TUNE WEBER & DELLORTO DCOE & DHLA CARBURETORS
- Updated & revised edition
by Des Hammill

ISBN 1 901295 64 8
Price £14.99*

A book in the **SpeedPro** series. All you could want to know about the world's most famous and popular high-performance sidedraught carburetors. Strip & rebuild. Tuning. Jetting. Choke sizes. Application formula gives the right set-up for *your* car. Covers all Weber DCOE & Dellorto DHLA carburetors.

CONTENTS
COMPONENT IDENTIFICATION: The anatomy of DCOE & DHLA carburetors • DISMANTLING: Step-by-step advice on dismantling. Assessing component serviceability • DIFFICULT PROCEDURES: Expert advice on overcoming common problems in mechanical procedure • ASSEMBLY: Step-by-step advice on assembly. Fuel filters. Ram tubes. Fuel pressure • SETTING UP: Choosing the right jets and chokes to get the best performance from *your* engine • FITTING CARBURETORS & SYNCHRONISATION: Covers alignment with manifold and balancing airflow • FINAL TESTING & ADJUSTMENTS: Dyno and road testing. Solving low rpm problems. Solving high rpm problems. Re-tuning.

THE AUTHOR
Des Hammill has a background in precision engineering and considers his ability to work very accurately a prime asset. Des has vast experience of building racing engines on a professional basis and really does know how to get the most out of a Weber or Dellorto carburetor. Having lived and worked in many countries around the world, Des currently splits his time between the UK and New Zealand.

SPECIFICATION
Softback • 250 x 207mm (portrait) • 112 pages • Over 140 black & white photographs and line illustrations.

RETAIL SALES
Veloce books are stocked by or can be ordered from bookshops and specialist mail order companies. Alternatively, Veloce can supply direct (credit cards accepted).

* Price subject to change.

Veloce Publishing Plc, 33 Trinity Street, Dorchester, Dorset DT1 1TT, England. Tel: 01305 260068/ Fax: 01305 268864/E-mail: veloce@veloce.co.uk

ALSO FROM VELOCE PUBLISHING -

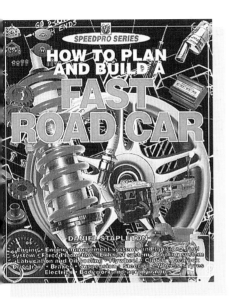

HOW TO PLAN AND BUILD A FAST ROAD CAR
By Daniel Stapleton

ISBN 1 874105 60 X.
Price £15.99.

A book in the **SpeedPro** series.

• For those wanting to make their go car faster the choice of components and modifications is bewildering - here, at last, is a straightforward guide.
• How to improve all four aspects of car performance - acceleration, braking, top speed and cornering speed - without wasting money.
• Clear, understandable style, with over 200 photos/illustrations.
• Applies to any road car.
• Contains useful addresses and contacts.
• An indispensable guide for *anyone* planning to modify their car for higher performance.

• Daniel Stapleton has written a number of magazine articles and books on the subject of high performance tuning/modification.

CONTENTS
Engine • Engine management systems and ignition • Fuel system • Forced induction • Exhaust systems • Cooling systems • Engine lubrication and oil cooling • Flywheel and clutch • Gearbox • Drivetrain • Brakes • Suspension and steering • Wheels and tyres • Electrics & instruments • Bodywork and aerodynamics • Index

SPECIFICATION
Paperback. 250 x 207mm (portrait). 128 pages. Over 200 mono photographs/illustrations.

RETAIL SALES
Veloce books are stocked by or can be ordered from bookshops and specialist mail order companies. In case of difficulty we can supply direct (credit cards accepted).

* *Price subject to change.*

Veloce Publishing Plc, 33 Trinity Street, Dorchester, Dorset DT1 1TT, England. Tel: 01305 260068/ Fax: 01305 268864/E-mail: veloce@veloce.co.uk

Visit Veloce on the Web - www.veloce.co.uk

Dune Buggy Handbook

The A-Z of VW-based Buggies since 1964

By James Hale

ISBN 1-901295-65-6. Price £19.99.

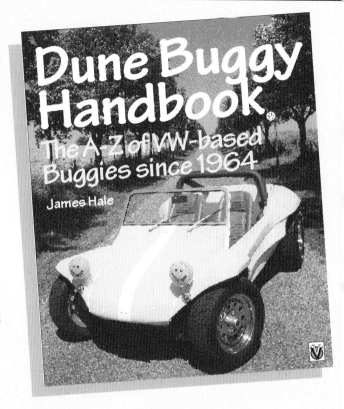

★ *At last! The complete A-Z guide to American & British Volkswagen based Dune Beach Buggies for all VW enthusiasts.*

★ Over 100 individual makes of Buggy described and pictured.

★ Each entry gives model description, identification tips & historical information.

★ Many previously unpublished photographs.

★ Written by a leading authority on Buggies, who also gives an introduction to the Buggy cult.

★ Contains archive material including period ads and sales brochures as well as related toys.

★ Contains an appendix detailing current manufacturers' addresses.

★ Not only has James Hale designed and produced Buggies for a leading manufacturer, he's also the resident Buggy expert for Volksworld magazine; his own car is a faithful reproduction of Steve McQueen's Thomas Crown Affair Corvair-engined Buggy.

CONTENTS

Foreword • Dune Buggies - cult transport for the young generation • A-Z directory: over 100 Buggies from past and present • Appendix: addresses of known manufacturers • Index

SPECIFICATION

Hardback. 250 x 207mm (portrait). 160 pages. Over 300 colour and black & white photographs/illustrations.

Volkswagens of the World
by Simon Glen

A comprehensive guide to all the Volkswagens not built in Germany, and the unusual ones that were. Includes VW type designations, chassis numbers, VW options, buggies, military, police, utility vehicles and all the lesser-known models produced by VW around the world.

Softback • 25x20.7cm • £16.99 * 176 pages • Over 650 b&w photos • p&p: £2.50/£3.50 overseas

VW Bus (Type 2 Transporter) Camper, Van & Pick-up
by Malcolm Bobbitt

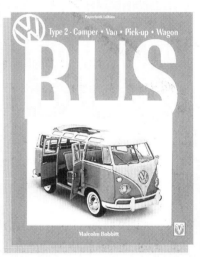

A revised paperback reprint at a bargain price. The full story of the Transporter from the earliest 'Split-screen' types through the 'Bay-window' models to the later 'Wedge' generation.

Softback • 25x20.7cm • £14.99 • 160 pages • Over 160 colour & b&w photos • p&p: £2.00/£3.00 overseas

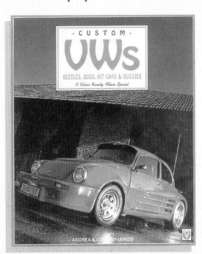

Together, these **Colour Family Albums** by Andrea and David Sparrow, are a celebration of the life and times of the Beetle, the VW Bus and all those customised VWs around the world, in superb original colour photographs combined with an entertaining, non-technical text.

Hardback • 25x20.7cm • £12.99
96 pages • 96 original full colour photos • p&p: £1.00/£2.00 overseas

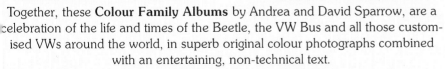

Visit Veloce on the Web - www.veloce.co.uk

Index

1300 Beetle 18, 21, 55
1302/03 Beetle 9, 18, 19, 20, 22, 48, 49, 50, 51, 67, 72, 77, 85
1302S/03S Beetle 18, 72
1500cc Beetle 17, 18, 21, 40, 43, 55
Accelerator cable 97
Adjustable spring-plates 60
Aeroquipe 48
Aluminium-bronze linkpin bushes 26
Anti-roll bar clamps 29
Anti-roll bar 29, 32, 33, 40, 41, 42, 80, 81
Anti-squeal shims 46
ATE 15, 24, 25, 35, 43, 45
Autocavan 4, 25
Avis adjusters 28, 52, 53, 54, 60
Axle gaiters 71, 72

Ball-joints/suspension 18, 23, 24, 25, 28, 29, 39, 40, 41, 42, 49, 51
Bernard Newbury 100
Bilstein 30, 31, 59
Black Diamond discs 44
BMW brake shoes 77, 78, 79
Braided brake lines 36
Brake hoses 63

Brake line clips 57
Brake proportioning valve 68, 80
Brembo calipers 48
Bugpack 29, 30, 31, 100
Bump stops 28, 57
Bump-steer 33, 34, 41

Cabriolet Beetle 22, 93, 101
Caliper rebuild 46
Calipers 43, 46, 79, 69, 70, 71
Cal-look 51
Camber adjustment protractor 13
Camber compensator 61
Camber 19, 56, 57, 60, 61
Castor angle 32
Castor shims 32, 53
CB Performance 24, 25, 41, 48, 49, 69, 70
Chassis 8, 14, 15, 63, 83, 84, 85, 86, 87, 88, 89
Chassis/cable shortening 86, 87, 88, 89, 90, 91, 92, 93
Clutch cable 98, 99
CNC 25, 99
Cofap steering damper 31
Copolymer 71, 72, 74

Copper brake pipes 36
Cross-drilled discs 25, 45
Custom & Speed Parts 24, 25, 35, 36, 48
CV (Constant Velocity Joint) 19, 57, 73, 74, 75, 78

De-cambering 56, 60, 63, 78
Diagonal A-arms 21, 71, 75, 76, 78, 79, 81, 95
Disc brakes 17, 18, 22, 24, 25, 26, 27, 35, 36, 37, 40, 43, 44, 45, 46, 47, 48, 49, 50, 64, 69, 70, 77, 80, 95
Disc pads 45
Dow Corning 75
Dr Ferdinand Porsche 14
Drag racers 32, 60, 61, 63
Drive shafts 57
Dropped spindles 24, 28, 35, 44
Drum brakes 15, 17, 24, 26, 27, 35, 36, 37, 38, 39, 42, 50, 51, 64, 65, 66, 67, 69, 71
Dual-circuit master cylinder 26, 27
Dune buggy 8, 9, 18, 33, 38, 59, 81, 84, 86, 87, 88, 101

Dura Blue 75

Eccentric camber bushes 41, 42, 44
EMPI 47, 61, 94, 100
Expanding parallel reamer 27

Fast road 58
Floorpans 14, 83, 89
Flop-stops 60
Ford Escort 60
Ford 25
Formula Vee 7, 8
Front suspension adjusters 28
Fusca Beetle 21

Gas Spax 59
Gear selector rod 87, 88
Gearbox straps 63, 64
Gearbox 16, 62, 63, 64, 71, 72, 74
Gene Berg Enterprises 29, 32, 52, 64,
   100, 101
German Car Co 69, 70
Girling 43, 45, 47
Golf GTi 24, 25, 68
Goodridge 48
GT Beetle 18, 40

Handbrake/cables 15, 17, 56, 57, 62,
   65, 67, 77, 78, 97
Heater cables 97
Hockey stick selector 62, 87
Hot rod 28
Hub bearings & seals 59, 65, 69, 70
Hurst 100
Hydraulic clutch 99

IMP 86
Inboard adjusters 60
IRS (Independent Rear Suspension)
   18, 19, 20, 21, 22, 23, 55, 60, 66,
   69, 71, 72, 73, 75, 77, 78, 81, 84,
   88, 92, 93, 94, 95

Jamar 25, 99
JaTech 24, 25
John Maher Racing 49

Karmann GF 86
Karmann Ghia 18, 40, 43

Kerscher 45, 69, 71
King & linkpins/suspension 16, 17,
   18, 23, 24, 25, 26, 27, 28, 35, 36,
   37, 41, 43, 49, 51
Kingpin inclination 32
Koni 30, 43, 59
Kubelwagen 18
KYB 30

Loctite 63
Long-travel ball-joints 41, 53
Lowered spring plates 60

MacPherson struts 13, 18, 20, 21,
   22, 49, 85, 86, 96
Master cylinder 17
Metwrinch spanners 12
Micarta bearings 32
Mini 29
Mole grips 13, 67

Neal 24, 25, 99
Needle roller bearings 32

Oil deflector 70
Oil flinger 70
Opel Kadett 29
Outboard adjusters 60
Oversteer 61

Pagid fast road pads 45
Pedal cluster 98, 99
Pickle fork 13, 42
Polyurethane bushes see 'urethane'
Porsche 356 36, 37, 38
Porsche 911 48, 73
Porsche 924 71, 73, 75
Porsche 944 45, 48, 49, 50, 71, 73,
   75, 76, 77, 78, 79, 80, 88, 94
Porsche Carrera 48
Porsche Speedster 84
Porsche Spyder 84, 86
Puma Beam 29, 39, 52, 54

Quickshift 100, 101

Race Spec 58
Racing-style clamp-nuts 36
Rack & pinion Steering 22

Roller pedal 99

Second World War 7
Select-A-Drop 28
Semi–automatic/stickshift 9, 19, 21,
   55, 72
Shifters 100, 101
Shock absorbers (dampers) 19, 29,
   30, 57, 58, 59, 63
Snap-On 12
Solid mounts 64
Spacers 47
Spax 30, 43, 59
Spectra Dynamics Deflex bushes 29,
   58
Speedy Cables 79
Sperwolf 101
Spring-plate retainers 60
Spring-plates 16, 19, 55, 56, 57, 58,
   59, 60, 62, 63
Standard model 15
Static negative camber 77
Steering gearbox 17, 23, 30, 31, 52
Summers Brothers 75
Sun Sedan 20
Super Beetle 20, 21, 22, 49, 50, 55,
   94, 96
Super duty mounting 64
Suspension stiffeners 93, 94
Sway-A-Way 28, 29, 40, 51, 52, 58,
   60, 61, 64, 75, 80
Swing-axle rear suspension 16, 19,
   56, 57, 60, 72, 73, 94, 95

Talbot Horizon 47, 48
Toe-in/out 19, 33, 56, 57, 60
Torque-Meister 12, 80
Torsion bar assembly (front) 28, 31,
   32
Torsion bars (rear) 16, 55, 56, 57,
   58, 59, 60, 61
Torsion leaves 16, 28, 31, 32
Toxic Shock 29, 30
Track rods/ends 17, 33, 34, 35, 43
Traction bar 64
Trailing-arm 30, 40, 42, 43
Transaxle straps 63
TUV 69

Urethane bushes & fittings 30, 32, 58, 59, 60, 61, 62, 63, 64, 77

Vauxhall Cavalier 25
Ventilated discs 45, 46, 50
VW 181 75, 79
VW Corrado 71
VW Discount 46

VW Golf 49, 69
VW Type 2 75, 78, 79
VW Type 3 37, 44, 48, 50, 51, 64, 66, 68, 71, 94, 95
VW Type 4 44, 48, 75

West Coast Metric 101
Wheel bearings 35, 36, 38, 39, 44

Wheel cylinders 17, 37, 38, 65
Wilwood calipers 24, 25

Z-bar 55, 57, 61
Zimmermann 45